D1036685

"If you want to know what it would have been like in ancient Corinth, spend a week in the life of a freedman, traverse the olive groves and cobblestone streets, survive the cutthroat politics of a Greek city, encounter pagan priestesses and converse with a Jewish tentmaker named 'Paulos,' then Ben Witherington has written the book for you. This short novella, with pictures and explanations of customs in ancient Corinth, provides a window into the world of Paul's Corinthian letters. Witherington creatively brings the setting of Paul's Corinthian ministry to life with historical rigor and narrative artistry. Witherington brings to us the sights, smells, sounds and culture of Corinth as the apostle Paul knew it."

Michael F. Bird, lecturer in theology and Bible,
Crossway College, Australia

"This book provides a uniquely enjoyable way to learn about ancient culture and Paul's mission in Corinth by immersion. Although I found the story delightful and intriguing, I could also see behind it careful research on a large array of details."

Craig Keener, professor of New Testament,
Asbury Theological Seminary

"This very readable—indeed, gripping—book gives us an imaginative insight into the Greco-Roman world of Paul's mission to Corinth. The details of everyday life for Paul and those he met are set in their historical context by an expert scholar who knows the New Testament and its background very well. I recommend it to all who want to understand the setting in which early Christianity grew and flourished."

Alanna Nobbs, professor of ancient history,
Macquarie University, Australia

"This imaginative narrative brings the New Testament world to life by following the freedman Nicanor around ancient Corinth, relating his encounters with religion, gladiators, politics, domestic life and the nascent Christian movement (including several biblical characters). Though it may not solve all the riddles of the Corinthian correspondence, here is an engaging and informative introduction to Corinth and the wider cultural context of the first-century Roman Empire."

Brandon D. Crowe, assistant professor of New Testament, Westminster Theological Seminary

"Like the valley of dry bones being covered once more with sinews and flesh, Corinth rises from its overgrown ruins to its former vibrancy, color and intrigue, allowed to re-live one week of its history. Witherington masterfully mingles the pleasant and the useful as he introduces readers to the social institutions, household customs and civic life of the Roman colony of Corinth by telling a delightful story centering on the attempts of one Erastus to win a public office and one Paul to prepare for his trial before the Roman proconsul, Gallio. I know of no other introduction to the Greco-Roman environment of Paul's mission that could also qualify as entertaining 'beach reading.'"

David A. deSilva, Trustees' Distinguished Professor of New Testament and Greek, Ashland Theological Seminary

A WEEK IN THE LIFE OF CORINTH

BEN WITHERINGTON III

IVP Academic
An imprint of InterVarsity Press
Downers Grove, Illinois

InterVarsity Press
P.O. Box 1400, Downers Grove, IL 60515-1426
ivpress.com
email@ivpress.com

©2012 by Ben Witherington III

All rights reserved. No part of this book may be reproduced in any form without written permission
from InterVarsity Press.

InterVarsity Press® is the book-publishing division of InterVarsity Christian Fellowship/USA®, a
movement of students and faculty active on campus at hundreds of universities, colleges and schools
of nursing in the United States of America, and a member movement of the International Fellowship
of Evangelical Students. For information about local and regional activities visit intervarsity.org.

All Scripture quotations, unless otherwise indicated, are taken from the Holy Bible, Today's New
International Version™ Copyright ©2001 by International Bible Society. All rights reserved.

Cover design: Cindy Kiple
Interior design: Beth Hagenberg
Images: antique frame: © Mr_Vector/iStockphoto
       Corinth Forum: © Balage Balogh/Art Resource, NY

ISBN 978-0-8308-3962-9

Printed in the United States of America ∞

 green
press
INITIATIVE
As a member of the Green Press Initiative, InterVarsity Press is committed to protecting
the environment and to the responsible use of natural resources. To learn more, visit
greenpressinitiative.org.

Library of Congress Cataloging-in-Publication Data

Witherington, Ben, 1951-
 A week in the life of Corinth / Ben Witherington III.
   p.cm.
 ISBN 978-0-8308-3962-9 (pbk. : alk. paper)
  1. Paul, the Apostle, Saint—Fiction. 2. Corinth (Greece)—Fiction.
3. Bible. N.T.—History of Biblical events—Fiction. 4. Christian
saints—Fiction. 5. Apostles—Fiction. I. Title.
  PS3623.I865W44 2012
  813'.6—dc23

                                              2012000268

P   23 22 21 20 19 18 17 16 15 14 13 12 11 10 9 8 7
Y   34 33 32 31 30 29 28 27 26 25 24 23 22 21 20 19 18 17

CONTENTS

1

POSEIDON'S REVENGE

♦ ♦ ♦

The late winter sun was already warming the chilly Mediterranean air as the ship approached the harbor on the incoming tide. You could just make out the very top of the Acro-Corinth, the ancient acropolis where the temple of Aphrodite stood, towering over the city and majestically rising above the morning mist. The captain had offered the morning sacrifice, a young sea bird caught at dawn, and the auspices were propitious. All hands were on deck, carrying out their orchestrated tasks as the captain bellowed orders. And the passengers did their best to stay clear of the action.

Nicanor had seen enough sea voyages for a while. His poor stomach felt like it had swallowed half the Adriatic Sea, which he had just crossed on his way back from Roma. He had fallen into a pattern of only eating later in the day from the stock of dried fish he had brought with him from Roma. He was regretting his spare diet. Next time he would bring a slave to do the dirty work of cooking and cleaning instead of trying to economize.

No wonder his former master and present employer, Erastos, had sent him, rather than going himself to transact

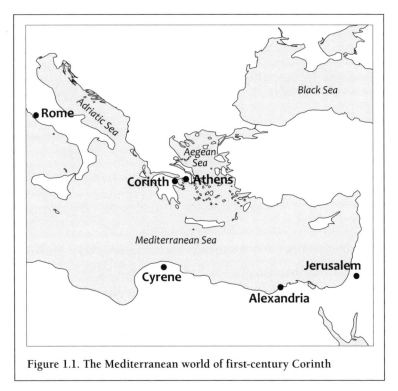

Figure 1.1. The Mediterranean world of first-century Corinth

this business deal. Besides, no one should have to sail the
Adriatic in the first week of *Februarius*, not even former slaves.
The fact that it was *Dies Lunae*, the Moon's Day (that is,
Monday), reminded Nicanor of the effect of the moon on the
tides. This was not the first time he had acted as the "agent"
of Erastos, and doubtless it would not be the last. But next
time he would remember to ask that tasks like this be undertaken during the proper sailing season, after the middle of the
month of Mars and before the end of the year, when the
weather changed. Despite his queasiness, a smile crept across
Nicanor's face when he thought of his success in bargaining
for additional Carrera marble for the building project Erastos

♦ A CLOSER LOOK ♦

Slaves and Manumission

The Roman Empire was not merely dependent on slave labor, it was largely built on the backs of slaves. Slavery was a burgeoning enterprise. Estimates suggest that up to half the population of Rome, the Eternal City, were slaves. This is not totally a surprise, for the more territory Rome took over, the more prisoners from all walks of life and social status they took, and the more people were turned into slaves. We must resist the temptation to equate ancient slavery with the antebellum slavery in nineteenth-century America, though there are some analogies. One striking contrast is that some of the most highly educated and brilliant persons of the Roman Empire, and some of its best businessmen, were or had been slaves.

Corinth, due to its location, was a clearing-house for the slave trade, and the wealthy in Corinth were able to buy the best slaves available in its slave market. The slave, by the definition of Aristotle, was a piece of living property, but property nonetheless. As such, slaves had no legal rights whatsoever and were subject to the will and whims of their masters. There is some evidence that in Paul's day there were attempts to ameliorate the absolute power owners had over their slaves, as a result of concerns about slave revolts, like that of Spartacus.

No one, not even the slaves who led slave revolts, was arguing for the abolition of slavery in the Empire. Slaves wanted to be treated fairly, and many of them wanted their freedom and were able, with their masters' help, to buy their freedom. There are even slave inscriptions that say "slavery was never unkind to me" (CIL 13. 7119). The legal vehicle by which a person like Nicanor could be set free was called the *peculium,* which allowed slaves to accumulate both property and money, and indeed earn enough to pay for their manumission. But one's master, in this case Erastos, had to agree to the manumission. A slave had no legal recourse if the master refused his request for manumission. When Paul says in 1 Corinthians 7 that if the slave has the opportunity to become free, he should take it, he is not referring to a situation that the slave himself could initiate. It was the master's choice.

had undertaken. This was strategic in Erastos's plan to procure the office of *aedile* in Corinth.

Nicanor could hardly complain, for he had finally had the opportunity to see Roma for an extended period of time. He had never seen such a huge city before, with people literally living on top of one another in neighborhoods called *insulae.* And, of course, it was always fascinating to see how another race of people lived. For instance, Roman men, unlike the Greeks, were clean shaven and paid a visit to the barber regularly, where gossip abounded. And among the new things Nicanor had discovered during his days in Roma was the Romans even had a religious ceremony called the *depositio barbae,* in which a teenage boy had the fuzz removed from his face for the first time! Romans seemed to be a more religious and less skeptical lot than many of the Greeks Nicanor knew in his homeland, but some of that religion seemed like mere superstition.

On the other side of the coin, there were things Nicanor saw that his father, a Greek teacher and sometime philosopher, would have called lurid, indicating the Romans were less morally refined than Greeks. Nicanor remembered being asked by his father to memorize a rhetorical speech by a Roman about Roma, which said in part, "Yet the characteristic vices peculiar to our city seem to me to be inculcated almost in the mother's womb, that is the enthusiasm for acting, and the passion for gladiators and racing. In a mind preoccupied and obsessed by such things, what little space is left for the higher arts?"[1] Nicanor had certainly heard much in the eateries, or *tabernae*, of Roma to confirm the Roman enthusiasm for such coarser forms of entertainment.

♦ A CLOSER LOOK ♦

The Roman Calendar

In 45 B.C. Julius Caesar had regularized the Roman calendar by adding extra days so that the months would not get out of sync with the seasons. Caesar inserted sixty-seven days between November and December. Thus the Julian calendar divided the year into exactly twelve months, to which was added a Leap Day in February of every fourth year. On average therefore, the Julian year was 365.25 days long. Today we follow the Gregorian calendar because a solar year, which determines the season's cycles, is about eleven minutes shorter than 365.25 days. The problem with the Julian calendar was that these extra minutes led to a gain of almost three days every four centuries. And this eventually set it clearly at odds with the twice-yearly observed equinoxes and thus the seasons. The Gregorian calendar was not proposed until the sixteenth century. And it handled this problem by simply deleting some

---

[1]This is in fact a quote in Tacitus's famous *Dialogue*, 29.3-4, from a slightly later point in time during the first century, but it is representative of the lament heard going all the way back to Augustus about how Rome was degenerating morally, as was reflected in its choices of entertainment. Nero in fact in the 50s made it acceptable for even the elites to prefer this sort of entertainment.

calendar days so that the calendar would once more be synchro-
nized with the equinoxes. Later, the Gregorian calendar also
dropped three leap-year days, once every four centuries.

Surprisingly, even into the twentieth century the Julian calendar
remained in use as a civil calendar in some countries before being
replaced by the Gregorian calendar. In the ecclesiastical world the
Julian calendar was replaced by the Gregorian calendar in both the
Catholic and Protestant Churches. However the Orthodox Church,
except in Estonia and Finland, retained the Julian calendar for calcu-
lating the dates of moveable church feasts. Interestingly, the Julian
calendar is still used by the Berbers of North Africa.

On the horizon Nicanor could just see the *diolkos*, the rutted
road that began at the western port and headed across the isthmus.

Figure 1.2. The diolkos

Though they almost
looked like ants from
this distance, Nicanor
knew that what he saw
gleaming in the sun
were the bare-backed
slaves dragging a small
boat on a sledge the two
miles across the isthmus
on the diolkos, a short-
cut that avoided the sail
around the whole of
Greece to get to the
Aegean Sea. While he
was in Roma he had

heard the rumor that the new emperor, young Nero, had ambitious plans for Isthmia, including the digging of a ship canal through the two miles of the isthmus. That ought to upset Poseidon a bit, not to mention the merchants who made their fortune hiring out teams of men and sledges for hauling boats.

Figure 1.3. The Corinth Canal

Figure 1.4. A Roman-era stone sarcophagus from Sinop, Turkey. Its side contains a relief of a merchant ship and a harbor boat.

Standing in the bow of the *Romulus and Remus*, a medium-sized grain freighter some one hundred feet long, Nicanor clung to the rigging that ran down to the prow. He could now begin to make out the details of the temple of Aphrodite on the huge Acropolis hovering over the bustling city of Corinth, a city that had become the hub of the Roman province of Achaia. The city had come a long, long way since it was largely destroyed by the Roman general Mummius over two centuries prior. Who could have guessed that the Roman soldiers who were mustered out of the army and given land would simply blend in with the largely Greek culture here? True enough, they had imposed their own legal system as an overlay on the culture. But you could hardly tell the Romans from the Greeks anymore. They had intermarried, they all dressed in the same style, and the Romans had adopted the Greek dining and festival customs. Despite Latin being the language of the courts, the language on the streets for everyone was Greek.

Nicanor was only twenty-seven years old, but already he had begun to make a decent living as the freedman of a man on the rise in Corinth—Erastos was himself the offspring of a Greek mother and a Roman centurion who had mustered out in Roman Corinth during the reign of Augustus. But Erastos had a secret, a secret he did not want spread abroad as it would ruin his chances to become aedile, the office that included the tasks of being the city treasurer and public works supervisor. Erastos had become part of a new religious cult in town that met privately only in people's homes.

Nicanor, whom Erastos trusted implicitly, had actually been present at one of these meetings, and it was most strange. What sort of religion met under cloak of darkness in a home, and

♦ A CLOSER LOOK ♦

The Destruction and
Romanization of Corinth

In 146 B.C. the Roman general Mummius destroyed the ancient city of Corinth, leaving only the ancient temple of Apollo standing. According to reports, the women and children were sold into slavery, and the statues, paintings and works of art were seized and shipped to Rome. Corinth was then mostly reduced to ashes. What arose thereafter was a city largely designed on a Roman plan and serving Roman legal and military purposes. Even so, the native Greek culture and language remained dominant, not least because the Romans were outnumbered in the region by native Greeks. Latin was the language of the law, the courts and official public inscriptions, though Greek seems to have been used for most everything else. Everyone could speak Greek, and perhaps most could also use Latin. Some Jews from the East would have also been able to use Hebrew and Aramaic.

Corinth remained largely depopulated for about one hundred years after the destruction by General Mummius. It was Julius Caesar in about 44 B.C. who made ancient Corinth into the Roman colony city of Corinth, *Colonia Laus Iulia Corinthiensis*. The Romans in general were recyclers—they used the ancient Greek designs in rebuilding the city, though the organization and street plan varied a little from the ancient city. The city Paul and Erastos knew had had a stable and growing character for over a century. Indeed, by the 50s, the town, with its two ports and active slave market, had become the epicenter of trade going both east and west in the middle of the Mediterranean.

Not surprisingly, Roman colony cities favored Romans when it came to matters of property and justice. Roman soldiers were mustered out into such colony cities (Philippi was another Roman colony city), and there was a dominant Roman layer of society at the top of the social and governmental structure in Corinth. Since Paul appears to have been a Roman citizen, and Erastos certainly was since he could run for the office of aedile, these two men had certain natural and legal advantages in a Roman colony city. This is probably why Paul's legal case with the Jewish leaders was thrown out of court.

without priests, temples or sacrifices? And then there was all that singing and apparently some kind of prophesying, and then a sort of fervent speech in a language Nicanor had never heard before or since. It had given him chills when he heard it, and he wondered if the participants had given way to the sort of mania one associated with the oracle at Delphi after she had chewed the sacred leaves.

He knew, of course, that the religions that originated in the eastern end of the empire were odd. Take the Egyptian rites of Isis and Serapis, and the so-called mystery religions. What really went on behind those closed doors, and why were the sexes segregated in that worship? And then there was the religion of the Jews. How in the world could anyone think there was only one god, especially when you lived in the land of Mount Olympus? But Nicanor had to admit that these religions seemed almost normal compared to what seemed to be the credo of this Eastern religion Erastos now embraced. The credo was explained in the rhetorical discourse he had heard that night in the house of Erastos by a man with an oddly Eastern accent, a small balding man named Paulos. There was something about a crucified Jew and that he should be worshiped. This stretched credulity past the breaking point.

Nicanor had a decision to make. Marcus Aurelius Aemilianus, the other candidate for aedile, had approached Nicanor. Over glasses of the finest Falernian wine, Marcus had told Nicanor he could advance his own career in a dramatic fashion if he would dish some dirt to him about Erastos, dirt he could use to publicly shame the man and cause him to lose the election. It was evident that Erastos was the leading candidate and Aurelius was struggling to catch up. But Aurelius had one great advantage—he was as rich as King Croesus and could buy many votes from ordinary citizens. The election was not for another month or so. But Nicanor had been offered enough money that he could begin to afford to build his own villa, expand his business, even perhaps marry a higher status woman in Corinth! It was a temptation most former slaves would not be able to resist.

But Nicanor was a different sort of person, a person of principle and ethics. His late father, Heraklidos, had been a *paidagogos* and even a tutor for wealthy children in Athens. Before the Romans had conquered his home city of Aphrodisias and enslaved him, Heraklidos had been a well-known Stoic philosopher and teacher. Prized for his knowledge, wisdom and ability to read and write in several languages, Heraklidos had been hauled off to Corinth and sold in the slave market for a substantial sum of silver *denarii* to a rich family in Athens.[2]

The world of slaves and slave dealers was a shameful one. The slave markets were auctions run by aediles of the city. These

---

[2]In fact, such a slave could cost as much as several thousand dollars.

public officers set the terms for the auctions—the place, rules
and regulations. Around each slave a scroll was hung bearing
their name, national origin, and a statement of their health (diseases and conditions such as epilepsy were expected to be noted)
and character. Was he prone to theft or flight or taking his life?
That would be noted. This declaration constituted a "guarantee"
that was good for six months. Within that time limit, if a clear
and unmentioned defect showed up, the dealer was obliged to
take back the slave. Slaves with no guarantees were distinguished
by a special cap on their head. Slaves imported from the provinces carried a tax and were distinguished by having their feet
whitened with chalk. They would be examined by their buyers,
of course. And exceptional slaves—particularly those who were
remarkably attractive—might be singled out for private sales to
worthy clients. Slaves were property, the trade was profitable and
the sale of female slaves for sexual trade was common.[3]

Nicanor had vivid memories of that day. The tears flowing
down his father's cheeks, dripping onto the scroll hung 'round his
neck. And then the slave dealer's shout, "He's sold!" Nicanor had
watched him being dragged off, put into a cart and trundled to a
destination unknown. You don't forget those kinds of traumatic
events, and quietly it had made Nicanor wonder why in the world
a good man like Erastos would ever want to become an aedile if it
meant presiding over such a brutal and inhuman process.

As often happened, Heraklidos's children were also sold, but
to a different family, the family of Erastos. Nicanor had been
taken from his father when he was only seven and had never
seen his father again until the week he died. As he mulled over

---

[3]For more on this, see the article on slavery at <www.classicsunveiled.com>, from
which this information was culled.

these painful memories he wondered just how much loyalty he really owed Erastos. Even for Nicanor the pull of temptation was strong, to take revenge, to throw himself in the arms of Nemesis and strike back against the family who had ripped him from the arms of his father those many years ago. But he must not act in haste. It would be dangerous to set in motion the spiral of negative payback so ingrained in his culture just when he was beginning to make his way in the world. He must weigh his options carefully.

The blast of a trumpet suddenly jolted Nicanor out of his contemplations and signaled that the good ship *Romulus and Remus* was finally rounding the breakwater at the harbor, leaving the choppy seawaters behind. The sails rattled and slumped down the mast, the tow boat stretched the line taut, and the ship eased into the harbor. As the dock lines were cast and the boat was pulled into its moorage, Nicanor said a silent prayer of thanks to Poseidon for the safe sea voyage. But his stomach reminded him that he had eaten very little for well over a day now.

The weak winter sun warmed his shoulders as he clambered down the gangplank, carrying only his shoulder bag with a few traveling possessions. The fog was gently lifting from the hills on the left, where the road to Corinth could be found. On the dock there were *amphorae* of wine just unloaded. Sailors, just given leave, were heading immediately for the dockside *tabernae*. Roman soldiers kept watch over the toll collector's booth. A garment salesman offered fresh tunics and togas to the dirty disembarking souls. And prostitutes were hanging about with knowing smiles, hoping for some early morning business.

Compared to the salty tang of the clean sea air, Nicanor was immediately struck by the stench that emanated from and hovered over the dock and shore. It was not merely the stench of those disembarking the boat, but the strong smell of sweating human flesh, of rotting garbage and of the overripe scraps of seafood from the fishmonger's stall, even as he unloaded a fresh catch from a little boat not ten feet away.

Clashing with that, and just as potent and pungent, was the smell of the small spice market across the way. There every manner of myrrh, frankincense, anointing oils, pistic nard and other fragrances were available. Some of the newly disembarked would head straight to this shop before heading inland. Knowing they did not have time to bathe or clean up, they chose to overpower their stench by hanging a little vial of nard or some other potent fragrance around their necks. Pistic nard was very expensive, the most expensive of the perfumes, and yet you would never know it on this day as it was selling rapidly to the more wealthy of the newly landed residents and tourists. Nicanor made a mental note—here was another little business he might invest in one day.

Grabbing a small loaf of bread and some olives and figs from a street vendor only one hundred yards from the dock, Nicanor began his walk toward the villas that lay nestled on a hill between the old city of Corinth and the Acro-Corinth. It was a cloudless sky, and thus far everything augured well for Nicanor. It was only the first hour of the day and so the early morning business trade was in full swing.

Nicanor realized he was already a day or so late, and Erastos would be anxious to hear the outcome of his transactions, for Erastos was a punctual man who at that very hour would be finishing up dealing with the queue of slaves, "friends" and clients who had begun lining up outside his door at dawn. Thereafter he would be off on his horse checking his vineyards and olive groves. Nicanor must catch him before that happened. Picking up the pace, while wolfing down his bread and few olives, a smile crept across Nicanor's face. It was good to be back on dry land again, very good indeed. But it was almost a ten-mile hike from where he was to Erastos's house, and he needed to get a move on.

2

ISTHMIA AND ITS GAMES

♦ ♦ ♦

Nicanor had been gone just long enough to have entirely forgotten how soon the preparations would begin for the biannual Isthmian summer games. Among other things, the games meant considerable business opportunities for Nicanor as the tourists began coming to the region, renting tents and camping out near the site of the temple of Poseidon. Nicanor had two small businesses. He ran a taberna in Isthmia, a small eating and drinking establishment that would be flooded with customers this summer during the games. He also had a small construction firm that was currently employed repairing the aqueduct on the back side of the Acro-Corinth. On top of all that, he continued to serve as a business agent for Erastos, though he wondered how, with his own businesses beginning to thrive, he would be able to continue tending to Erastos's affairs.

These were heady days in Corinth and its surrounding villages. Ever since Corinth had been named by the Romans as the capital of the province of Achaia, it had been stealing not only the thunder from Athens, but a lot of business as well. When the center of political power shifted, shrewd businessmen

knew that the center of trade would follow. Nicanor was riding
the swelling tide of this business boom.

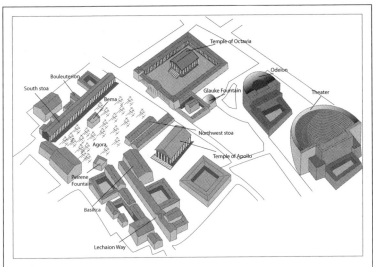

Figure 2.1. First-century downtown Corinth

Figure 2.2. A view of Corinth from the temple of Aphrodite

Everywhere one looked there was construction going on,
and as Nicanor was passing the ancient temple of Poseidon at
Isthmia he noticed yet another dining room structure being
erected adjacent to that temple. If time had allowed, Nicanor

would have visited the temple and left a small thank offering for safe passage over the seas. But there was absolutely no time for that today. Likewise he would have visited the public baths, as the stench of wearing the same unwashed clothes for days and days was upon him. But, he figured, that very odor would tell Erastos that Nicanor had been diligent and had come in all haste, tarrying for nothing.

Nicanor was a man on a mission, and he found himself traveling in the company of one Krackus, an enormous hulk of a man with olive-colored skin and bulging muscles. He was a well-known gladiator who trained and fought in all the arenas of Achaia. Standing some six feet five inches tall, he towered over Nicanor, who even by Greek standards was a small man, at about five feet three inches. Krackus was as friendly and unassuming as any giant could be, and Nicanor had enjoyed striking up a congenial conversation as they walked toward Corinth.

"So how many times have you fought in the arenas of Achaia?" asked Nicanor.

"I'm in my thirty-third match, and as you can see here on my left bicep, I've got the wounds to show for it. No one has yet defeated me, even with a trident and a net. I realize, however, that I am on the downside of my career. I've made enough money that I don't have to do this anymore, especially since last year I purchased my freedom from Alexandros, who owns the school of the gladiators just over the hill there."

Nicanor gave Krackus the once-over and noticed various scars on his rippling biceps, and especially on his enormous left thigh, as thick as a giant fir tree, where an injury had produced a slight limp. It was indeed about time for Krackus to get out of the fighting business before he lost all his agility, never mind his nerve.

"So, Krackus, would you be interested in a new job, working for me, after your next confrontation in the Isthmian games? I could use someone to police my taberna here in Isthmia. I can provide decent living quarters, all the wine you could drink and all the food you could eat."

"I wouldn't be too hasty in making that offer, good sir—you haven't seen me eat or drink! I wager I could consume all your profits pretty quickly!" said Krackus with a hearty laugh. "But still, it is an offer worthy of consideration, and I will think on it. I would welcome less travel and fighting in my life, and it would be good to settle down and perhaps even have a family. I imagine there are a few women in Corinth who still fancy gladiators?" With this comment Krackus winked and rolled his eyes.

Nicanor chuckled and replied, "More than a few, if you judge by the graffiti on the walls in Corinth. I saw a graffito a while back that read 'Andronicus is my hero, and I long for his powerful love. Daphne.' When the literate and educated women start writing epithets like that on the plastered walls of Corinth, you know you are popular."

The conversation continued for the next twenty minutes or so until the two men reached a fork in the road. Krackus headed directly for the Lechaion Road to downtown Corinth, whereas Nicanor needed to veer to the left and go around the southwest corner of the city, then head up the hill toward the Acro-Corinth where Erastos's estate lay. "Well met, Krackus," said Nicanor. "May the gods protect and favor you in your next match. And do look me up at my shop in Corinth. You will recognize it from its sign with a picture of a Corinthian column on it. *Vale*."

The huge man with the olive skin and jet-black hair smiled and waved as he strode off to the right. Nicanor was excited about the

◆ A CLOSER LOOK ◆

Gladiators and
Their Contests, Part One

While the Greeks had long held various sorts of biannual and quadrennial games (e.g., the famous Olympic games), the addition of blood sports—mortal combat between men—was a more recent development as a form of entertainment that rose to great popularity with the growth of the Roman Empire. It does appear this was first an Etruscan sport passed on to the Romans, and not a sport that originated in the East. More clearly, the games reached their peak between the first century B.C. and the second century A.D. The gladiatorial games projected the message to peoples on the farther reaches of the Empire that Romans were fierce fighters, a message many had already received at the sharp end of conquering Roman legions. It may come as some surprise that these games and contests endured through the social and economic upheavals of the last centuries of the declining Roman Empire. And even after Christianity became a legal religion, and in due course the official religion of the Empire (and in fact Constantine banned the contests in A.D. 325) we hear of contests being sponsored by the Empire. The last known gladiatorial contests took place late in the fifth century A.D.

Most gladiators were slaves or soldiers taken as prisoners of war who had been trained under severe conditions, and most patrician Romans thought they should be segregated from the general citizenry. But this did not prevent some patrician and ordinary women from swooning over these stars of the arena. And across the Empire some gladiators who had retired from the arena reasonably unscathed became bodyguards for the wealthy.

By New Testament times gladiators had become big business for trainers and for owners. This was also the case for ambitious politicians on the make and for those who had already reached the pinnacle of the *cursus honorum*, the sequence of offices in a political career. A very ambitious private citizen might even postpone his deceased father's gladiatorial celebration until the election season so as to put on a brilliant spectacle and gain some votes. The truth was that both those seeking power and those in power needed the support of the plebians and their tribunes, who could be swayed to vote for someone who put on a spectacular show. As we shall see, Erastos's rival for the office of *aedile* was putting on games coinciding with his running for office in order to increase his popularity, whereas Erastos had decided to undertake a *leitourgia*, a "liturgy," or public works project, to garner favor and popularity.

possibility of hiring such a giant. Krackus by himself could assure that the atmosphere in his taberna continued to be friendly and safe for all comers and not degenerate into a place where only drunks and ladies of the night would want to fraternize. Whatever his fee, Krackus would be worth it, and as a former gladiator, he would attract some business from men who loved to chat endlessly about the games and the triumphs and tragedies of the arena.

Coming over a small rise, Nicanor came to a huge, cultivated olive grove. He noticed that already tiny green olive buds were beginning to appear. It would only be another month or so before the onset of the real spring growing season, for Corinth was surrounded on all sides by the warm waters of *Mare Nostrum*, as the Romans called it, "our sea." Unlike cities such as Delphi, well up in the mountains, Corinth enjoyed the benefits of the moderating sea breezes in the summer and the warming current in the winter. Coupled with its fertile soil, Corinth was not only a prime

♦ A CLOSER LOOK ♦

Gladiators and
Their Contests, Part Two

When the gladiators appeared in the arena, they wore as little clothing as possible so they would be agile. Here is a brief list of what you might see them wearing or carrying.

For clothing and protection:

♦ *subligaculum*: loincloth

♦ *galea*: helmet

♦ *manicae*: leather elbow or wrist bands

♦ *ocreae*: metal or leather greaves

♦ *parma*: round shield

♦ *scutum*: large oblong shield

For weapons:

♦ *gladius*: sword

♦ *hasta*: javelin

♦ *sica*: dagger

♦ *iaculum*: casting net

♦ *tridens*: three-pronged spear

The more popular types of gladiators were *equites*, who fought on horses; *bestiarii*, who fought animals; *essedarii*, who fought from war chariots; *retiarii*, who fought with a trident and a net; *sagittarri*, who were mounted bowmen; and *rudiarii*, who were free gladiators, such as Krackus, who had won or bought their freedom through remarkable performances.

Normally, gladiatorial games were linked with the fighting of wild beasts in the arena (see 1 Cor 15:32). No doubt some of the slaves bought and sold in Corinth were bought to be trained as gladiators. Surprisingly, sometimes free men, particularly the poor, would try to advance their lot in life through fighting. Why? Because anyone who joined a gladiatorial school would be provided with food, shelter, clothing, training, armor and weapons. Gladiatorial schools were often elaborate structures, such as the model of a famous one near Rome in figure 2.3.

Smart owners would treat their prized fighters well, no matter what their social origins, and gladiators customarily kept their prize money and any gifts they received. The Emperor Tiberius offered the staggering sum of 100,000 *sesterces* for the return of certain gladiators to the arena, and Nero is said to have awarded the gladiator Spiculus an estate "equal to those of men who had celebrated triumphs." It should not surprise us to hear that Mark Antony was known to appoint gladiators to his personal guard.

But most gladiators did not expect to survive the games. Indeed, they all swore an oath: "He vows to endure to be burned, to be bound, to be beaten and to be killed by the sword." Nevertheless, when the prize money was large, the fortunate gladiators were able to buy themselves out of their slavery and survive to live a long and normal life, providing their owner was willing to cooperate.

Figure 2.3. Ludus Magnus, the gladitorial training school of Rome

spot for merchants and merchandise, but also for all sorts of farming and crops. Chief among these were olives and grapes, but also a variety of grains such as wheat and barley. As much as Nicanor, a proud Greek, hated to admit it, he had good reason to thank the Romans for all the good roads they had paved, even in southern Greece. But there were roads and then there were roads. Some were major thoroughfares and relatively smooth; some were minor and unpaved. At the moment Nicanor was making excellent progress along the sea road that led from the isthmus along the coast, turning inland to Corinth itself.

◆ A CLOSER LOOK ◆

Roman Roads

The first type of Roman road, the *viae publicae regalesque*, were public and royal roads that were constructed and maintained by public funds. Such roads led to a town or to a body of water—a sea or lake or river—or joined up with another public road. These roads were under the authority of *curatores* (commissioners) and were repaired by *redemptores* (contractors). Beyond general public funds allotted for roads, tolls were extracted from travelers. The older roads tended to take their name from their destinations or the regions through which they passed. But a road might be renamed if the censor ordered major work on it, such as paving, repaving or rerouting. The Lechaion Road was, in fact, the original road to Lechaeum, but now bore a Romanized form of the name. In towns, a fixed contribution was levied from the neighboring landowners. In Rome, for example, property owners were responsible for maintenance of the streets that ran past their property. It is not surprising that people like Erastos felt they especially had the right to use such roads for commerce as well as travel.

Figure 2.4. Roman Road

Figure 2.5. Carriage

After another mile or two Nicanor found himself on a narrow path, too narrow for the wider Roman carriages of the wealthy. But there were still small carts being hauled along this path, and Nicanor found himself dodging to the right and left to get out of the way. At the same time he had to avoid stepping in deep ruts, an ever-present hazard that resulted in many a turned ankle.

What should he talk to Erastos about first? Well, of course, the business deal, but after that, what? Should he dare to broach the subject of Erastos's rival? Did he want to become the object of a sort of bidding war for his services? Would Erastos swear him to silence and eternal loyalty?

Nicanor could feel anxiety knotting his gut as he thought through these questions. He could find himself enmeshed in a dangerous and ruinous game, no matter which person he sided with. The conventions of enmity would kick in and he might find himself on the short end of the stick. Not to mention the possibility of landing in court before Gallio, the proconsul, who despised dealing with local wrangling. Here was a dilemma not easily resolved. He must tread lightly, step carefully and think hard.

3

PAULOS, PRISCILLA
AND AQUILA

♦ ♦ ♦

Paulos, the Jew from Jerusalem, was already sitting in his shop
on the Lechaion Road by the time Nicanor had alighted from
the grain freighter. An early riser, he did not sleep well due to
his various injuries over the years. And now he was hard at
work stitching away on a piece of *cilicium*, a jet-black goats'
hair cloth, named after the region of his birth, Cilicia. Unlike
the shops that were built into the front of city houses, Paulos's
rented space was in a structure designed only for business.
Built of stone blocks, the shop had an entranceway shaped like
the great arches that supported aqueducts. Hanging on the
walls and arranged around the shop were a variety of leather
products, including furs worn as outer garments in the winter,
"skins" for carrying wine, harnesses for horses, belts and, of
course, tents. The shop was actually rented by three persons:
Paulos, Priscilla and Aquila.

Paulos was born in Tarsus but raised in Jerusalem, and he
was a man of considerable social status. His parents had been

Figure 3.1. A shop off the Lechaion Road in Corinth

citizens of Tarsus, and as a result of providing the Roman army in their province with tents, they had become Roman citizens as well. Paulos knew that in a city like Corinth, having such status and citizenship could be a strategic trump card should difficulties arise over his orations about Jesus the risen Lord.

By now Paulos was a balding, middle-aged man. And in spite of his everyday tradesman appearance, he had been well-educated at the feet of Gamaliel and in the school of Greek rhetoric and philosophy in Jerusalem. He had now been bearing witness to Jesus' deity for over fifteen years. And the fledgling, factious and diverse Christian community in Corinth bore witness to his efforts. Now in his second full year ministering in Corinth, considerable inroads had been made both in the synagogue and also among the pagans. Indeed, all sorts of rumors were spreading around Corinth about the secret dinner-party meetings at which the followers of Jesus were said to eat his body and drink his blood. Some pagan residents had worried that it sounded like cannibalism. Was this yet another Eastern mystery religion of some sort? At the junction of two seaports, Corinth seemed to collect diverse religions like it collected slaves and ethnic groups.

Paulos often marveled at the variety of humanity in Corinth. There were persons of every skin color imaginable, from the darkest Ethiopian to the near lily-white northern Gauls who occasionally showed up in slave markets. But most bore a hue somewhere between the extremes, with the dominant skin color being tan or olive. What was interesting about all this was that while one's ethnic group or tribe certainly did matter to many, it was not skin color that served as the basis for pride or prejudice, by and large. Anyone from anywhere in the Empire could now be a "Roman" citizen if they met certain criteria, and Paulos reckoned there were as many persons who were not ethnically Roman or Etruscan who were Roman citizens as those who were! In his own lifetime, with the rise of the Empire, "Roman-ness" and even the word *citizen* had taken on a whole new and non-localized meaning.

The morning sun was shining into the south side of the shop, illuminating the stretching rack on which Paulos laid his tents to sew and work the skins into a particular shape. The Isthmian games were coming, and the tent trade was picking up. Paulos had a large order from a vendor who would be renting them out to those camping in a field right next to the site of the games. Even by a conservative estimate, the population of Corinth and Isthmia would double at the height of the games, and lots of temporary shelters would be required.

Paulos had been able to sustain himself by his leather working and tent making, in part through the help of his

♦ A CLOSER LOOK ♦

The Appearance of Paul

Figure 3.2. Fresco of Paul and Thecla

In the Syriac text of the second-century apocryphal document called the *Acts of Paul and Thecla*, Paul is described as follows: "He was a man of middling size, and his hair was scanty, and his legs were a little crooked, and his knees were projecting, and he had large eyes and his eyebrows met, and his nose was somewhat long, and he was full of grace and mercy; at one time he seemed like a man, and at another time he seemed like an angel." This description is the basis of the early drawing of Paul found in a cave above the city of Ephesus used for worship, high above ancient Ephesos. (See figure 3.2.)

We have no way of being certain about the accuracy of this physical description, and in any case, the function of such descriptions was to reveal something about the character of the man (hence the reference to "he seemed like an angel") more than the appearance of the man. In ancient iconography a high forehead would be a sign of wisdom more than just intelligence, and since eyes were seen as the windows of the soul in antiquity, large eyes suggested a large or deep soul to the ancients.

The physical description in the *Acts of Paul and Thecla* seems to also give us a stereotypical description of a Jewish man with a long nose and bushy eyebrows that met. Median height in Paul's age, for a Jewish man, seems to mean somewhere between five foot five and five foot ten. Paul was certainly no goliath, even by ancient standards. The crooked legs and protruding knees might be taken as the signs of a man long on the road, and aging rapidly. Whatever the actual appearance of Paul, this description is meant to convey the impression that Paul, by Jewish or Christian standards, was a saintly man, well travelled and wise.

ministry partners: Priscilla, a higher-status woman from Roma, and her husband, Aquila, from Pontus. These Jews had become followers of Jesus while they were in Roma, long before meeting Paulos, and when he came to Corinth looking for those who were also members of the leather-working guild, they met and immediately struck up a friendship. In A.D. 49 Priscilla and Aquila, along with other Jewish followers of Jesus, had been expelled from Roma by the Emperor Claudius. The reason was the controversy stirred up in the synagogues and Jewish community in Roma by those who were preaching about Jesus. Priscilla and Aquila had lived in Corinth for some two years, and Paulos had worked with them in their trade for the past year or so. On this morning, Priscilla was the second to arrive at the shop.

"Grace and peace, Paulos," said Priscilla as she walked through the entranceway in the third hour of the morning. Dressed in her neat, well-stitched, dark blue toga, with the top of the garment pulled over her head, this middle-aged woman looked every inch the *domina*, the patrician woman. In fact, she had been part of the Priscillan *gens* in Roma, but like quite a few noble Roman women, she had taken an interest in Eastern religions. First it was Judaism, which was a licit religion in the eyes of the Romans. Then she was attracted to the following of the Jewish messiah, Jesus, which some Jews and many Gentiles in Roma had embraced ten years earlier, long before any of the pillar apostles got to Roma. Priscilla had met her husband, Aquila, a traveling tent salesman from Asia Minor, at a synagogue in Rome. The danger of following the Jew Jesus was that if the Romans were to view that sort of religion as something other than a peculiar Jewish sect, its devotees would become fair game for persecution, prosecution and even execution as practitioners of an illegal religion.

"And peace to you, Priscilla," said Paulos with a smile. "I fear we shall be buried in making tents this spring. There will be little time for spreading the word about Jesus."

"Well, it's the price you pay for avoiding patronage, Paulos."

"You are right, of course. And I have had trouble explaining my refusing patronage to some of our well-heeled friends, Erastos for one. He just doesn't understand it. And he's frankly a bit upset with me for turning down his patronage. But I really can't afford to be bound by these reciprocal relationships. I can just see myself confined to Corinth as someone's paid after-dinner speaker!"

"Yes," replied Priscilla. "Not to mention that you need to get yourself ready to face Proconsul Gallio and the wrath of those

♦ A CLOSER LOOK ♦

Patrons, Clients and
Reciprocity Conventions

In the Greco-Roman world, social relationships worked differently than they do today in the West (and much more like they do in many non-Western cultures today). Reciprocity, or payback, was something that characterized relationships not only between patrons and their social inferiors, who were their clients, but even between social equals in business transactions.

Most patron-client relationships were euphemistically called friendships (*amicitia*). And this is apparently one reason Paul largely avoids using such language in his letters. It would have signaled that Paul and his converts were in a patron-client relationship. These sorts of social relationships existed because of the nature of ancient society and economic life. The society was highly stratified, with the upper 5 percent or so controlling the vast majority of wealth and the economy as well. This was especially the case in a Roman colony city like Corinth, where Roman laws and practices ruled. A social inferior, once he had become someone's client, was no longer free to come and go as he pleased. He was more like a hired hand. In a society where, by and large, it was patrons and not banks that loaned money, and where there was no adequate government social safety-net, patronage and clientage were necessary for the survival of many of those of lower social status.

So in Corinth Paul was diligent in avoiding "gifts" and patronage since they always came with strings attached. Because of the party spirit of the Corinthians, if Paul had accepted patronage there, he would have only exacerbated a spirit of rivalry. Patronage was not simply a matter of economic or social power and control. It was a matter of honor and shame, and even of spiritual or religious control. Paul had to tiptoe carefully through the minefields of this social network to make sure the gospel was not seen as a commodity to be bought, and its apostle was not seen as a gun for hire. In short, Paul avoided patronage for the same reason he was reluctant to use his Roman citizenship to further the gospel. In both cases, doing so just further inscribed the entrenched social hierarchies. By contrast, Paul believed that in Christ there is neither slave nor free, neither patrician nor plebian, neither Jew nor Gentile, and no male and female as well. All are one in Christ.

synagogue rulers in court. They feel you have shamed them. And no wonder! You converted not one, but two of their elders!"

"Right you are, Priscilla. As usual. I hope I don't have to play my trump card of Roman citizenship, like I did in Philippi." Paulos sighed, offering a somewhat sad smile to Priscilla, and then looked down again at his stitching. "How do you think Aquila is faring on his current business trip?"

"As you know, he insisted on traveling to Thessalonike by boat. But he should be working his way south by land this week. I dreaded the thought of him going by sea in Februarius, and I at least persuaded him to return overland, even if it takes longer. The thought of him traveling in one of those small coastal ships, tossed by the winter sea and in peril of running aground . . . I can hardly stand it."

"I confess that my mind has not been on his travel. I guess I have been too caught up in trying to make peace with our synagogue rulers. But they are not having it. I originally hoped to have Aquila carry and read out a letter to the brothers and sisters in Thessalonike. I guess I have been so focused on trying to sort out problems in our house churches, trying to get these tents made and preparing for trial, that the opportunity got away from me."

"You and I aren't getting any younger, Paulos," Priscilla retorted with a grin that revealed the wrinkles around her eyes.

The two friends were so engrossed in conversation that they hardly noticed the young man standing in the doorway with a rolled sheet of papyrus in hand.

"Excuse me, sir, are you Paulos of Tarsus?" he asked in a timid voice.

"That I am, lad. How can I help?"

"I have a document for you about the *actio prima* (the first part) of your trial. You are summoned to appear two days hence at the *bema* just down the road, before the Proconsul Gallio."

Paulos rose and took the document. Unrolling it quickly, he looked up and said, "Thank you, young man, you have discharged your duty. You may go. Tell them I will appear."

Paulos was well aware that in most Roman colony cities there was real animosity against Jews in general, and especially if they were troublemakers. The rumor was that Gallio was famously anti-Jewish, as the proconsul Pontius Pilate had been twenty years before when Paulos was in Jerusalem at the time of the crucifixion of Jesus of Nazareth. The only good news was that in this court case, both the plaintiffs and the defendant were Jews. Gallio would have no natural inclination to favor either side.

"Paulos, we must pray about the day after tomorrow. Shall we do that now?"

"Certainly, sister Priscilla, let me just sit down here, and let's do so."

The crowds passing down the Lechaion Road, shopping and conducting their morning business, hardly noticed the two middle-aged Jews quietly bowing their heads and lifting up holy hands as they said their prayers to the Lord Jesus, imploring him for help in the upcoming trial.

After their prayer, Priscilla was off to take care of some shopping and errands, leaving Paulos to his work. His calloused and aging hands skillfully stitched the thick leather, forming a tent seam. His eyesight, a persistent problem, was a nuisance to someone who worked with his hands. But with his back to the shop entrance he was able to catch the morning light on his work and make steady progress on a tent he had been working on for a few days.

"Excuse me, Paulos," said a familiar voice over his shoulder. "Have you a moment?"

"For you, Stephanos, my friend, of course I do." Paulos rose and embraced the man whose whole family had embraced Christ over a year ago. Paulos had baptized them in the sea at nearby Cenchreae, the eastern port of Corinth, where Phoebe and other followers of Christ lived.

Sitting down on the vacant stool next to Paulos, the congenial Jewish man began to ask, "Can you help me to better explain to some of our Jewish friends the idea of Christ's death on a cross being an atonement for sin? They are not used to thinking of crucifixion, or for that matter the shameful death of a human being in general, as being the way to cleanse us from sin."

Paulos turned his stool so he could face Stephanos and look him in the eyes at close range. Then he began, "I realize it is a scandal to most Jews to talk about a crucified messiah. Indeed it sounds like a contradiction in terms. But let us think for a moment about what the prophet Isaiah said about God's suffering servant . . ."

♦ A CLOSER LOOK ♦

Paul, a Visionary
with an Eye Problem

To judge from Galatians 4:15, Paul seems to have had eye problems. After telling his converts in Galatia that he had come to their region due to an illness, he then adds, "You would have torn out your eyes and given them to me." If the eyes were the windows of the soul, and a man came with some sort of noticeable eye disease, this would suggest to many that he had a troubled soul. Indeed, he might be the kind of person who could cast the evil eye on someone. Paul says that the Galatians had received him as if he were an angel, even though his condition put them to the test. They had not spit (to ward off the evil eye) nor scorned him, but received him as they would have received Jesus. Perhaps eye problems were Paul's thorn in the flesh, which might explain why a physician like Luke would be a welcome companion. It would also explain why Paul signed his name in very large letters (Gal 6:11). Perhaps Paul's eyes never fully recovered their health after he was blinded on the Damascus Road.

The issue of Paul's eyes is important because for an orator like Paul, one's physical appearance was crucial in establishing ethos or authority. In 2 Corinthians 10:10, Paul repeats the Corinthian criticism that while Paul's letters are rhetorically weighty, his appearance was weak and his speech contemptible. The latter is probably a comment on Paul's accent, which would not have come across as good Attic pronunciation and intonation of the Greek, but rather as Eastern Greek. "He appears weak," they complained. This could refer to visible wounds (perhaps the possible stigmata of Gal 6:17), but more likely refers to some obvious physical weakness. There is something contradictory about a person who claims to be a seer, and who has had visions of heaven, but who has oozing eyes. And one who claims to perform healing miracles (Rom 15) ought not to need healing himself. In short, Paul had some hurdles to overcome as the apostle to a Gentile world that was saturated with rhetoricians and apt to judge orators by their appearance.

4

THE HOME OF ERASTOS

♦ ♦ ♦

The sun had not yet broken the horizon, but the household of Erastos was alive with activity. Slaves were up before daylight preparing food, sweeping the entranceway to the villa, feeding animals, polishing the front-room furniture where guests would be received, and cleaning the leaves and debris out of the *impluvium* near the entrance. And at the very back of the house, beyond and below the main garden, slaves were washing and bleaching the clothes, using the cleaning agent of choice, human urine.

The early part of the workweek was always hectic since various tasks Erastos would assign took several days to accomplish. This explained the long line of clients, slaves and business partners already assembling at dawn outside the front door. In any case, Erastos was an early riser, and so the door of the villa always opened precisely as the day began with the sun rising over the Acro-Corinth. Dressed in his best white toga, his curly hair combed into place and carrying a wax tablet inscribed with his to-do list, Erastos, together with his scribe Tertius, was prepared to face the day and its challenges. He began by sitting down in

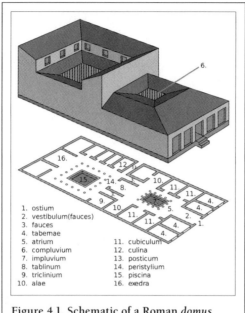

1. ostium
2. vestibulum(fauces)
3. fauces
4. tabernae
5. atrium
6. compluvium
7. impluvium
8. tablinum
9. triclinium
10. alae

11. cubiculum
12. culina
13. posticum
14. peristylium
15. piscina
16. exedra

Figure 4.1. Schematic of a Roman *domus*

the *tablinum*, prepared to deal with those waiting at the door.

But even before dawn, Erastos had spent some time with the Lares, the protective deities who in Roman and Greek religion were seen as guardians of the home and hearth. Though Erastos had recently become a follower of the Christ, old religious habits died hard. Erastos found himself comforted by the paired statues of these deities that his parents and grandparents before him had venerated as part of their morning devotion.

At this point Erastos had ceased venerating the Lares as gods and instead used that sacred spot in the house to ask the one God for guidance and protection for the day. Erastos had to admit that religious life was much easier when there was only one God who might bless or correct you, only one God to consult about life's important matters. A no-nonsense person,

Erastos found the Jewish religion made much better sense.
There were no more unknown gods. Indeed, any other spiritual
forces in the universe, though real, were not gods at all and did
not deserve to be worshiped. This Erastos had already come to
believe during his time spent in the synagogue before Paulos
came to town preaching Jesus, the crucified one.

Erastos's beautiful Roman wife, Camilla, was also already
busy, getting the domestic servants in line and on task for the
day. Erastos now needed to do the same. Sitting down at his
desk in the tablinum, with Tertius sitting beside him, stylus
and wax tablet ready in hand, Erastos spoke to his doorman,
"Eutychus, it is time to let them in. Please open the doors."

A huge double door opened inward, bathing in light the area
where the master of the house and his scribe sat. In front of the
tablinum was the *atrium*, and in the center of the atrium was
the impluvium, where the rainwater came in through an
opening in the roof and was caught in the sunken rectangular
pool, where it would be available for various household purposes. Beyond the impluvium were the doors, and when they
opened, the parade began.

The first of the free persons to enter were clients, who circled
the impluvium and headed for the tablinum. They would be followed by freedmen, like Nicanor, then by the slaves who worked
the estate. With these latter it was Tyche's task to provide those
who worked in the vineyards and olive groves with both a work
list and with *sportulae,* lunch baskets with bread, wine, figs,
olives and nuts for the day's work. Erastos was well aware that
"man [particularly young agricultural workers] cannot live by
bread alone," so he tended to feed his servants better than his
fellow estate owners in and around Corinth.

"Vale, Erastos," said the first client of the morning. Standing before Erastos was a small wiry man named Cato, a Roman friend who had been mustered out of the Roman army, and now was trying to find his place in the world. While he had been granted a bit of land and a beast of burden, as well as a small stipend, Emperor Claudius had not been as generous in the allocation of pay for retiring soldiers as some previous emperors, like Augustus. And so Cato had found himself in the awkward place of nearly starting life over in Corinth. Thus far he had managed to till his land and buy a couple of slaves, but there was much to do, and he needed a loan to get a vineyard planted on the back side of the Acro-Corinth and to start an olive grove.

"How are you this morning, friend?" asked Erastos with a smile. "And how can I be of service to you?"

"I need a substantial loan so I can get on with cultivating my fields and producing fruit. I hate to ask for so much, but in all honesty, I need at least ten thousand denarii just to make a good start. Is this within the realm of possibility?"

Erastos scratched his head for a moment and said to Cato, "Why don't we start with five hundred denarii and see how far that will go? If it goes well, you can always come back to me again, and we can talk some more."

Cato sensed that now was not the time for haggling, and it would be better to get closure on this much money than to walk away empty-handed. Extending his right hand to shake on the deal, he replied, "Very well, Erastos, but don't be surprised if you hear from me again, sooner rather than later."

"Naturally I am looking forward to your success in this venture, and also your support as I run for the office of aedile. Anything you can do on my behalf before the election would be greatly appreciated."

♦ A CLOSER LOOK ♦

The Coin of the Realm

The ancient economy was not a money or free-market economy like ours. Rather the system of trading or bartering, yet another form of reciprocity, still held sway, though in Paul's day the economy was increasingly influenced by money. Money in an ancient economy was usually reserved for paying taxes, tolls and temple dues if one was part of the 95 percent of the population that was not wealthy. Money itself was minted by rulers, and increasingly by the emperor alone. It was a form of propaganda proclaiming who the so-called divine ruler was, and what some of his values were.

While the bronze *as* was perhaps the most common coin of the Roman Empire, and one of little value, the silver *denarius* became the most widely used coin by the middle of the first century A.D. One denarius, in 2010 dollars, was worth somewhere around twenty U.S. dollars or a bit more, so in the story, Cato is asking for a very large sum indeed, $200,000. The silver denarius became the standard daily pay for a day laborer who worked between ten and twelve hours on an estate in a given twenty-four-hour period.

Figure 4.2. An *aureus*, a Roman gold coin worth twenty-five denarii

The nature of imperial propaganda, focused on the emperor himself, can be seen in the picture and title appearing on the Nero coin in figure 4.2. Nero is depicted as having won the laurel wreath at the games in Isthmia or elsewhere, in this case for poetry. Below is a coin from the exact period when our story transpires, during the close of the reign of Claudius, whose demise came in A.D. 54.

Figure 4.3. Roman denarius depicting Claudius

Under the Empire the actual silver content of the denarius was about fifty grains, or 1/10 troy ounce. In 2010 this would have corresponded to approximately U.S. $2.70 in value if the silver was 0.999 pure (which it wasn't). For more details, see the article "Denarius" in *A Dictionary of Ancient Roman Coins* by John R. Melville-Jones (1990).

Cato smiled, said, "Of course," and the deal was consummated. The next hour and half was taken up with lesser transactions, and Erastos was a little puzzled by this. He wondered if Marcus Aurelius Aemilianus was siphoning off some of his "friends" in the run up to the election, currying favor with them. He made a mental note to have one of his servants do a little checking in the forum to see what Aurelius was up to. Erastos had a premonition he was up to no good, as was his way. He was not exactly a man who modeled the virtue of *pietas*, much less honesty.

Figure 4.4. Corinth's forum

At the third hour precisely, Erastos finished his business at the house and headed off to the back side of his estate to check on the aqueduct. Water had been flowing only sporadically through the pipes on the estate, and something was awry. There had been plenty of rain this winter. His servant Loukas had run to the stable and prepared the master's horse, as he wanted to get out to the aqueduct and back quickly. It crossed his mind that Nicanor should be arriving soon from Roma, and Erastos was anxious for a full report. The fate of his *liturgy*, his public works project, hung in the balance, and so too his being elected to the office of aedile.

Kissing Camilla chastely on the cheek, he said, "I'll be back soon. Heading out to the aqueduct to see what has happened to the water flow. Something's amiss." She waved as he mounted his horse and rode off into the morning sun, which by now was just overhead to the left at about a forty-five-degree angle. It promised to be a bright and beautiful day.

About an hour after Erastos had left, up the path to the front door trudged Nicanor, tired, dirty, and carting a large pack with his belongings in it. Little Julia, Erastos's daughter, now seven, saw him coming from her upstairs bedroom and ran down to the door. She insisted Tyche open it, and then flew down the path and right into the arms of Nicanor.

"Where have you been so long, Nicanor? My lessons have been neglected and the paidagogos just keeps repeating the same old dull paradigms and rhetorical models for me to practice. It seems like ages since you left!"

Reaching down and picking up Julia, Nicanor ruffled her hair and said, "I've been away on business for your father, you know. All the way to Roma and back."

Nicanor had spent much of his time as a slave tutoring Julia and her two much older brothers in reading and writing Greek, as well as the *progymnasmata*, the elementary exercises in speech and logic and a bit of philosophy. Julia was becoming one of the brightest and most well-educated children in all of Corinth, especially among the girls. Erastos and Camilla had agreed that all three of their children should receive the same education, and Julia, a surprise child who came later in life, was the apple of her father and mother's eye, the little princess of her family.

"Is your father at home?" asked Nicanor.

"No," the little voice sweetly replied, and then in a more adult tone added, "I am afraid he left a bit ago. Something about checking the aqueduct."

From the doorway Camilla appeared, and approaching with a smile, she gave Nicanor the kiss of greeting.

♦ A CLOSER LOOK ♦

Home Schooling
Greco-Roman Style

The term *paidagogos*, which is the basis for the English term "peda-gogue," in fact does not refer to a teacher per se. The paidagogos is the slave who acts as a child minder, walking little Publius back and forth to school, protecting him, and then helping him recite his *alpha, beta, gammas* when he gets home. When Publius comes of age, he can leave the nanny, the child supervisor, behind. This does not mean he would stop his education, because, again the paidagogos is not really the educator, but more like a parental figure who helps with the homework and child care (see Paul's use of the term in Gal 3:24).

What did a Greek or Roman elementary education look like in Paul's day? Besides reading and writing and basic literacy in Greek, the *progymnasmata*, or what could be called by Paul the *stoicheia*, or elementary teachings, included grammar, geometry, astronomy, music, elementary philosophy and, perhaps more than anything else for the male patrician child in this oral culture, rhetoric, the art of speaking well and persuasively (see e.g., Philo, *Congr.* 11).

In one sense, ancient education used the same tools as were used in elementary schools as late as the 1950s with only slight variation. Rote memorization was the heart and soul of ancient learning, and while an American child sixty years ago may have practiced words and geometrical patterns with chalk on little blackboard slates, a child in Paul's day practiced on an ancient equivalent, using a stylus on a wax tablet or the like. The equipment of education only changed drastically with the advent of the computer age, and interestingly so did the pedagogy, with much less memorization being required.

What role did parents play in their children's schooling? If a parent could afford not to have the child working in the family business, and so go to school, then the parent could also afford a paidagogos, who was a slave, and provided educational assistance on the cheap and in the home. Some patrician or wealthy Roman matrons would teach their daughters how to spin wool and other similar domestic tasks. In general, "public education" was for boys, and domestic education for girls, but some Greco-Roman parents, like Erastos and Camilla, were more enlightened.

"We are so glad you have returned safely. We have been praying for that, and getting more anxious. What's the news about the marble?"

Nicanor tried to look downcast, then glanced up with a wry smile and said, "Only good news. The marble has been purchased at a fair price, and will be on a ship heading this way in a few weeks, once the weather turns for the better in early March."

"Please don't go chasing after Erastos," urged Camilla. "You need a bath, some good food and some clean clothes. Immediately!" Nicanor knew there was no gainsaying the mistress of the house—she was de facto the *oikonomos*, ruler of the house, with the consent of her husband.

"Since you insist," he said. "It's good to be on *terra firma* once more, and to be home." And with that, the three of them went back inside the villa as the morning sun rose in the sky.

5

THE ENMITY
OF THE ENEMY

♦ ♦ ♦

Marcus Aurelius Aemilianus was no ordinary patrician Roman. He was a direct descendant of the former dictator Sulla, infamous for using brutality to enforce his own version of martial law on a reluctant Roman people. Aurelius was a student of military history as well as his family's history, and one of his mottos about the climb up the *cursus honorum*, the ancient Roman equivalent of the ladder of success, was "by any means necessary."

On the surface Aemilianus seemed to be just another ambitious Roman with a pedigree. Because of his considerable wealth, he rarely needed to show his real colors. He could pay others to do his dirty work, and he was a master of manipulation. What better way to humiliate an opponent than to seduce his wife, shame him into retreat and perhaps run both the husband and wife out of town with gossip about their weaknesses or infidelities? Citing the example of Julius Caesar, who was famous for using this tactic, Aemilianus saw himself as a "ladies' man," and when it suited him, above the law. He did not cavil at breaking the law and then hiring the best lawyer money could buy to get him off the hook.

Aemilianus, largely due to his propensity to drink too much, had a memory like a sieve. So, like others of his means and vices, he had a *nomenclator*, a slave with a huge memory for names and details that Aemilianus could not be bothered with as he was a "great man" and such details were beneath his *dignitas*. The nomenclator, however, was a very sharp, keen-eyed, witty man who had come from the northernmost part of the Empire and so was called Britanicus. He was famous for his encyclopedic knowledge and made it his business to remember not only the names of every client and acquaintance Aemilianus met, but all of the particulars of Aemilianus's varied business deals. Thus he had managed to make himself indispensible to Aemilianus's lifestyle. In his spare time he also served as a tutor for Aemilianus's children, who were fascinated with his pale complexion and startling blue eyes.

On this morning Britanicus was giving Aemilianus a wide berth as the master's anger was readily erupting in the direction of whoever was closest to hand. It seems that on the previous afternoon, Aemilianus's favorite lamprey, kept in his back garden fish pond, had died. And that despite the best efforts of his keeper to feed and care for him. Like many uber-wealthy Romans, Aemilianus raised and bred his own fish, mainly bream, turbot, eels and lamprey, and just yesterday "Gargantus," Aemilianus's prized four-foot-long lamprey, had headed off to Hades. Britanicus knew that this morning was the wrong morning to bring up any troubling news.

Whether in the courts or in the business world or in politics or in the bedroom, Marcus Aurelius sought to dominate his opponents by whatever means he could employ. And now he had a largely unsuspecting and overly trusting Erastos in his sights, especially since Erastos had already declared he was a candidate for the office of aedile. Aurelius knew how to set the conventions of enmity into motion as well. And he was about to unleash this weapon on Erastos, beginning with the little scheme at the aqueduct he had already set up. Sending his largest slaves as his thugs, Aemilianus had them weaken and then break one of the tributary channels off the main aqueduct, the one sending water toward Erastos's villa and fields. But this was only his opening salvo.

Aemilianus knew that Erastos would personally go out and check the aqueduct. That was the kind of person he was—very hands-on, working even harder than his slaves and clients. Aemilianus figured a little rough stuff might rattle Erastos's cage a bit, inciting enmity and perhaps causing Erastos to overreact and come off as someone who could not master his emotions.

In the mind of Marcus Aurelius, Erastos had already offended him twice. First, by refusing weeks earlier the offer of his loan to help repair the aqueduct. Erastos had said no politely, that he could handle it himself. But then the enmity became even more intense when Erastos dared to run for the same office that Aemilianus had his sights set on and regarded as rightfully his. Thus the enmity conventions were doubly in play, and Erastos had best watch out for Nemesis.

Gratia, Aemilianus's wife, was what one might call a "kept" woman. She was rarely seen in public, and then only at necessary public functions with her husband. She was also a woman who had been unable to produce an heir. But for two good reasons, Aemilianus was not in a position to divorce her.

♦ A CLOSER LOOK ♦

On Finding Nemo—The Enmity Conventions

Going well beyond the modern spirit of competition and rivalry in sports are the ancient enmity conventions. Seneca, the Stoic philosopher and advisor to Nero in Paul's day, warned "You must be on your guard lest friendships be changed into serious enmities (*gravis inimicitias*), which are the source of disputes, abuse and invective" (*De amicitia* 21.78). Indeed such behavior could rapidly escalate into assaults on another man's person or family. One of the most dangerous things a person could do was to refuse a gift from a social superior or at least, in the case of Aemilianus, someone who saw himself as a social superior to the half-Greek, half-Roman Erastos, for Aemilianus was pure-blooded Roman with an infamous genealogy.

Rivalry or enmity conventions played themselves out in several arenas—families would compete in business, in politics, in athletic contests and in public works projects. When there was a political breakdown, such as when Julius Caesar was assassinated, there could actually be civil war between patrician factions. Besides the social conventions, there was also the belief in the goddess Nemesis. The Greek words *nemesis/nemo* refer to the dispensing of what is due, or the one who does such dispensing. Nemesis was a goddess who was often depicted with either a sword or a balance in her hands. She was also called *Invidia*, "jealousy," or even *Rivalitas*, "rivalry."

The goddess Nemesis was particularly associated with indignant retribution directed against those who committed evil deeds or were unworthy of their good fortune. She personified that deep-seated resentment aroused against those who committed crimes with impunity and got away with it, or who experienced the windfall of inordinate and undeserved good fortune. Nemesis was believed to have the power to direct human affairs in such a way as to maintain equilibrium. Tyche (fortune) was the god who doled out extravagant favors, so Nemesis was her negative counterpart, fulfilling the role of an avenging or punishing deity.

To couple the enmity conventions with a religious belief like Nemesis was a volatile cocktail. This was embodied in a person like Aemilianus, who saw himself as the human agent of Nemesis, avenging his own perceived slights or wrongs and visiting mayhem on others—in this case Erastos.

First, she was a member of the Julian gens, which connected Aemilianus directly to the Emperor Claudius, whose family he dared not offend. Second, she was extraordinarily and independently wealthy, and the dowry agreement had been clear. If there was a divorce, Gratia and her money left together. Indeed, even in the event of her dying before Aemilianus, the Julio-Claudians had insisted that the price of Aemilianus marrying into powerful connections was that he inherit none of their money when Gratia died. Aemilianus could use what money he needed while they were married, but he could not garnish her initial dowry nor expect to inherit her largesse. He was stuck and, in his mind, making the best of the situation. His sexual needs could be satisfied with regular visits to a high-priced *hetaira*, or "companion," who even accompanied him sometimes to the cruder blood sport contests, which Gratia abhorred. Aemilianus barely avoided being abusive at home when he was sober, and Gratia knew to hide herself away or visit a friend when he was drunk, for he was apt to rage against the unfairness of life and his having no male heir. All in all, Aemilianus was a nasty piece of work.

On this night, the second day of the week, the main meal had begun late in the afternoon and run well into the evening, as Aemilianus was entertaining clients. The *gustatio*, or appetizer, had come first, consisting of a small cup of honeyed wine and canapés. The main course that followed included a feast of meats—wild boar, chicken, turbot and, as a special delicacy, cow's udders and vulvas marinated in a special sauce. The meats of course were accompanied by the usual marinated olives, figs and dates. The dessert course was both shellfish and fruit, but in small proportions, as the drinking party was to follow for an hour or so. On this night a humorous old rhetor named Alexander had told several rich tales and then had concluded with a compelling speech on the virtues of competition. When the guests had finally left, Aemilianus was left alone with his thoughts, for his wife, Gratia, had retired with the rest of the women before the drinking party began.

Aemilianus, sipping his Falernian wine, wondered aloud to himself, "What shall I do about an heir? I am not getting any younger. I need someone sharp, literate, intelligent, a good businessman. I wonder . . . I wonder, perhaps I could make a young man like Nicanor my son? He is certainly sharp. I must speak with him soon and rachet up my offer if he will dish dirt on Erastos." Mumbling these schemes to himself while drinking mulled wine, a devilish smile crept across his face.

"Wouldn't it be sweet if I humiliated Erastos in more than one way and all at once—by stealing his client and former slave, Nicanor, and then thoroughly trouncing him in the election for aedile? There is nothing more delightful than shaming one's opponent from stem to stern." Then a frown crossed his brow, and he added, "It's a shame, though, that Camilla would repulse my advances. She's a woman who can't be compromised. Sadly, as she is quite fetching." On that note, Aemilianus succumbed to the sleep that had crept up on him unawares. His chief body servant, Didius, found him sprawled across his couch in the *triclinium*, snoring away and dreaming of the women he would yet conquer.

6

GALLIO'S GALL

♦ ♦ ♦

Junius Annaeus Gallio, a Roman Spaniard, had been proconsul
of the senatorial province of Achaea now for some months, and
it had gradually dawned on him how life in Corinth was rather
different from life in Spain. The son of Seneca the Elder, a
famous rhetorician, and the elder brother of the Stoic philosopher Seneca, who was later to be the advisor to Nero, Gallio
had not worked his way up the *cursus honorum* the usual way,
going from triumph to triumph, from smaller successes to
bigger ones. Indeed, at one point he and his brother had been
banished to Corsica and only brought back to Roma in the later
years of Emperor Claudius. He was lucky to have gotten the
post of proconsul over the newly formed province of Achaea,
which had Corinth as its administrative center.

Gallio had been known early in life for his charming
manner, at least according to both Seneca and the poet Statius.
And honestly, he wasn't much the governing type. He hated
all the tedious administration involved, and on top of it all, he
seemed to be allergic to the whole environment in Corinth. As
a result, he just couldn't keep himself well or in good humor.

Some of the local physicians had said that he was ruled by his bile or gall and that his humors were out of balance. They recommended blood letting, which Gallio emphatically rejected. These Greek doctors would stop at nothing to get paid a higher fee.

On this midweek day, Gallio was looking over the docket of his court cases and noticed that on the morrow he must deal with a Jewish dispute. Gallio, like most Romans, had little taste for Jewish squabbles and little patience with their religion, which to his mind was akin to atheism, since they believed in no gods but their own singular deity. But he had to put up with such folk since Judaism had been recognized by Augustus as a licit and legal religion of venerable antiquity. Sighing as he chewed on a date, he tried to get himself geared up for the sort of ridiculous pettiness he would have to deal with tomorrow. Today, however, he just couldn't face it. Instead, he was going to go to the temple of Asclepius for a luncheon. He would dine, meet some colleagues and friends, hear the latest news from the ports as well as the latest gossip and in general fritter away his day.

Leaving his house fairly early in the morning, Gallio went first to the more elite *thermae*, or public baths, to visit the toilets, work out briefly in the gymnasium and then work his way through the baths with their hot, tepid and cool pools. He would then have his skin scraped and his hair trimmed. Afterward he would go forth to the basilica to attend to some legal matters, thence on to the temple of Asclepius, the god of healing.

The temple of Asclepius was not far off the Lechaion Road, and without question, apart from the temple of Aphrodite on the Acro-Corinth, it was the most visited and popular temple in town. At

◆ A CLOSER LOOK ◆

The Baths, Part One

Figure 6.1. Caldarium (hot plunge bath) in Perga

The Greek word *thermos*, from which the English word is a transliteration, means "hot." From antiquity and on into modernity people have gone to hot springs to bathe, and indeed to get well. The term *thermae* came to refer to such places, and in the Roman era things were organized to the nth degree, with three separate pools often in three different rooms: the *cauldarium*, or hot water bath, the *tepidarium*, or lukewarm water bath, and finally the *frigidarium*, or cooling-off pool. In an age before most homes had indoor plumbing, the public baths were connected to the public toilets and sometimes also to the public gymnasium as well, making up a large complex of buildings. The ideal situation was that the baths would be built at or near a hot spring, but this was not everywhere possible, so the Romans devised their own hypocaust system of heating water underneath a tile floor, and turned the hot room into a steam room. Almost all Roman and Roman colony cities had such facilities, and this included Corinth once it became a Roman colony city during the reign of Julius Caesar in the first century B.C. In Corinth's case, we know of no hot springs, so the aqueduct supplied the water, which then had to be heated.

In some ways the more elite men's baths became a sort of gentlemen's club, where they would meet and sit around in the nude in the steam room (or with only towels of a sort), and discuss politics, personal issues, business deals and the like. Jewish males were at a decided disadvantage in such a setting due to their circumcision, which was ridiculed by pagans, and in some cases, we even know of Jewish athletes who went through a painful process of reverse surgery, reattaching or stretching a foreskin, so they could compete in the Olympic-style games in the nude without being the butt of jokes. As the Empire grew, these bath and exercise complexes grew larger and larger. Figure 6.2, for example, demonstrates the bath complex at Pompeii.

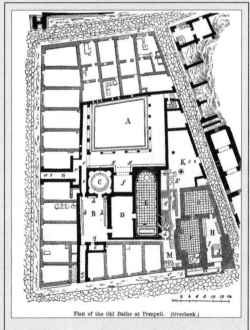

Figure 6.2. The old baths at Pompeii

Figure 6.3. Asclepius

Figure 6.4. Terra cotta votives

the entranceway up into the temple, beside the first stairway stood a new stone stele, with an image of both the god and the symbol of the god Asclepius, the snake entwined around a staff.

Gallio was late for the dinner party, and he hurried up the stairs into the temple, racing past the room with the terra cotta votives. Here were models of the various body parts pilgrims had used as offerings and prayers for healing. Gallio barely registered the familiar array of arms and legs, but the most common body parts replicated, male and female genitalia, caught his eye as usual. Grunting, he murmured to himself, "As they say, 'Not for every man is the journey to Corinth.'"

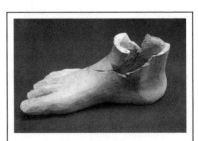

Figure 6.5. Terra cotta votive

The *triclinium*, or dining room, was on the back side of the Aesclepion, and Gallio could already hear the loud talking and revelry that accompanied such convivial occasions. Already present at the dinner was Aemilianus, who in Gallio's view was loud and obnoxious and full of himself, when he wasn't busy sucking up to Gallio for this or that favor. Deliberately avoiding the couch next to Aemilianus, Gallio positioned himself on the couch at the head of the rectangle, right next to the one that bore the statue of Asclepius himself. The belief was that the god dined with his companions whenever they visited his temple, and so there was always a prayer and small offering to the god before the festivities began. Only this time everyone had waited for the proconsul to begin.

The priest of the temple, Thucydides, asked Gallio, "Would you do us the honor of making the offering to the god?" Gallio nodded in response. Pulling his toga up over his head, he accepted with his right hand the little dish with a small portion of meat on it. The room fell silent as the priest called in a strong voice, "*Tacit!*" ("Be silent!") Heads were bowed, and in the best Greek he could muster, though with a Western accent, Gallio said thanks to the god for his many benefactions, healings and this very meal, and invoked him to be present with the diners. Gently placing the small dish on a little marble table beside the god's couch, and with as much decorum as was needed, the priest then said, "The god is pleased. We may begin the feast." What followed was some two and a half hours of reclining, then dining, followed by the *synposion*, or drinking party. The after-dinner speaker for the synposion on this day was the ever-popular Aeschines, a rhetorician of no little power and force. Today he would offer an entertaining epideictic encomiastic

speech, by which is meant a speech of praise or blame that
would laud some virtue or critique of some vice in dramatic
and hyperbolic terms.

The meal, or *cena*, began in earnest and would be followed
by the *convivia*, these being the Roman equivalents of the Greek
deipna (main course) and the *synposion*. In truth, Gallio, who
was no extrovert, did not like these dinner parties with their
disorderly conduct and displays of excess, their extravagance
and plotting, the sexual dalliance with the slave girls who
served the food and all sorts of posturing and bombastic re-
marks about politics and life. It was particularly in the drinking
party following the meal when things degenerated with the
flow of wine.

Gallio ate quietly while those around him made ribald
jokes, spit out food into collecting bowls so they could gorge
themselves with more and generally made themselves obnoxious. He was thankful these meals tended to reflect the
pecking order of society, with the most coarse and plebian
members of the party dining farthest away from the host and
chief guest, and in fact eating lesser quality food. Recently
Gallio had heard an epigram from one of his fellow Spaniards,
a younger contemporary named Marcus Valerius Martialis. It
amused him so much that he had memorized it. It was the
lament of someone having to dine at the bottom of the triclinium. It went like this:

*Since I am asked to dinner . . . why is not the same dinner served
to me as to you? You eat oysters fattened in the Lucrine Lake, while
I suck a mussel through the hole in the shell. You get mushrooms
while I get hog funguses. You tackle turbot, but I brill. Golden with
fat, a turtledove gorges you with its bloated rump, but a magpie*

*that has died in its cage is set before me. Why do I dine without you,
Ponticus, even though I am dining with you?*[1]

Thucydides, reclining on the couch facing Gallio, noticed
the grin shaping on his face and tried to strike up a conversation. "So, my lord, you seem merry this afternoon. May I
know the reason?"

"Oh, I was just remembering something funny, an epigram
told by Marcus Valerius Martialis." Gallio proceeded to quote it
to the priest in full, in Latin. Alas, this Greek priest knew little
Latin, and missed the humor. But he smiled and nodded politely, and so the conversation died almost immediately. The
meal was in any case drawing to a close. And just in time the
wine steward, the key player in the next part of the dinner
party, the convivia, showed up.

In Greece the wine server was a young, sexually attractive
teenage boy, catering not just to a taste for wine but to peder-
astic lust as well. This sad figure was dressed like a woman,
kept beardless and had the hair plucked from his legs. Gallio
remembered what his brother Seneca had said about this sort of
poor servant: "He is kept awake all day or night dividing his
time between his master's drunkenness and his lust." Gallio,
like his brother, had no time or stomach for such debauchery,
as common as it was. He had imbibed enough Stoic philosophy
from his brother.

Thucydides clapped his hands and said, "And now it is time
for our after-dinner oration by Aeschines."

Standing now in the middle of the triclinium, a short man
with dark curly hair and a closely cropped beard raised his hand

---

[1]This is one of Martial's famous epigrams—3.60.

toward the host, palms up, and in a clear, bell-like tone began:

"Noble friends, Romans, fellow Greeks, I am delighted to have the honor to speak to you on this august occasion, and knowing that you are keen consumers of the art of persuasion, I will endeavor to mold my speech not merely to entertain you but to please you. So it is that I turn to my theme, 'in praise of food and eating.'

"Though some have said 'we eat to live', no doubt you have noticed that there are some amongst us of notable girth who, seeking to disprove that theory, seem to believe 'we live to eat.' Their life seems to revolve around food, and so as the Greek philosophers have said, while some men are ruled by their minds, and some by their emotions, and some by their genitals, there are still others who are ruled by their stomachs. Oh, if only the belly could talk, imagine what tales it would tell about its obese master. It might say . . .

"'Lo, for these past sixty years I have been asked to work hard, taking into myself some sixty thousand meals. Yes, sixty thousand! Just when I think I will be given a rest, here comes some more food down the gullet, and does anyone ask me if I am ready for more? No indeed! It's just down the hatch we go, except of course when my master decides he really wants to indulge, in which case I am asked to send the food back up again, so even more can be crammed into my small quarters. And let me tell you I have seen everything—chickens, pigs, birds, fish, even dog meat once—yuck! And then there all the nuts, fruits, vegetables and sweets. Cakes of all sorts, pies of every description. I have sampled everything between Thessalonike and Sparta! Indeed, I could publish a guide to Greek cuisine thanks to my master's lust for food. For without cavil, my master lives to eat. It is his favorite activity. Even sex takes a backseat to eating. But I will whisper to you a small secret, if you promise not to tell. Though my master thinks he has control and rules me, in fact the reverse is true. Though I am by no means the largest part of his body, it is I who guides and goads him into most all of his plans and activities. As you can see, it is I, the stomach, who does all the talking, and my master obediently listens, day after day.'"

This entertaining speech went on for some thirty more minutes, with Aeschines graphically describing all sorts of sumptuous foods of Greece, so that while the first part of the speech, with its personification and "impersonation" of the stomach produced laughs and guffaws, by the end of the speech the audience was drooling over the imagined foods, so vividly had Aeschines described them all. Then he worked his way to his peroration . . .

"Gentle listeners, I have taxed your patience—or at least your palette—too long this day, so let me draw to a close. If you love food as I do, and if you live to eat as some do, then surely it must follow that more important to life than politicians, or rulers or slaves or beautiful women or doctors, are cooks and the culinary arts and the food that they produce. For while we can go weeks without hearing a political speech [some said "hear, hear" at this juncture], and we can go weeks without women when we serve in the military, and we can go weeks without slaves to answer our beck and call, and we can go most of a life without a doctor, is it not true that we can hardly go a day without food? If our need to feed is the most important need to stay alive and indeed to enjoy life, who can gainsay the conclusion—cooks should be our kings and good food our credo, for as one sage said, 'Man cannot live by mere bread alone.' Or as Epicurus himself once said, 'Eat, drink, and be merry, for tomorrow we may die!'" And at this the whole party raised their wine goblets and cheered.

After politely greeting a few people, Gallio waddled out the door of the temple, heading for home, his belly heavy with food, his head fuzzy from too much wine, and his gall bladder sending pains shooting through his upper abdomen as it worked overtime to produce bile. The sun was descending to the horizon on this midweek day, and the evening chill could already be felt. "Back to hearth and home, and rest . . . For tomorrow will be a busy day."

7

ERASTOS GOES MISSING

♦ ♦ ♦

Camilla was not a naive woman. Indeed, she understood the ways of the world quite well. And her instinctual radar had already gone off. Erastos had left that morning, and it was already past dinnertime. Normally, Erastos would have sent back a servant to tell Camilla he would be late getting home. And standing beside her in the atrium was a worried little girl saying, "*Mater*, where is *pater*? Should he not be here by now?"

Nicanor for his part was sound asleep in his old room near the back of the house. Having cleaned up and eaten in the middle of the day, Morpheus, the god of sleep and dreams, had wrapped Nicanor in his arms, and for six hours he had slept like a little child, without a care in the world. The toll of the rough voyage and the anxiety over getting home safely had caught up with him.

Camilla hated to bother Nicanor, but there was no one, including her most trusted slaves, whom she had more confidence in than Nicanor. Quietly walking through the atrium and toward the back garden, then taking a right, she came to Nicanor's quarters. She hesitated for a moment, listening at the door before she knocked. Then, with Julia beside her, she did knock, and heard a groan in response. Without warning, Julia burst into the room and pounced on Nicanor's bed, "Please get up. My pater is not home."

Groggy, and coming to slowly, Nicanor sat up in bed and said softly and slowly, "What?" Julia grabbed his hand and starting tugging on it, trying to get him up.

"It's true," said Camilla, standing in the doorway holding a hand lamp. "He left early this morning before you arrived, and he should have been home some hours ago."

Now fully awake, Nicanor did not like the sound of this. Erastos was nothing if not punctual, and always courteous enough to send a messenger if he was to be later than expected. He loved his family too much not to do so.

Standing up quickly and pulling his woolen cloak over his tunic, Nicanor prepared to take charge. "Call your three strongest and most reliable field workers. They should know the way to the aqueduct shunt, even in the dark. I want four good lamps as well, and a spare vial of oil. Get Xerxes the physician as well, just in case. We will set out at once." Striding through the courtyard, he looked up and noticed it had just begun to rain. "Great," said Nicanor to himself. "Just what we need right now. A trek in the dark in the rain."

A worried look creased Camilla's pretty but pale face. "Please be careful. As soon as you learn something, send a runner back to let me know what has happened—or if you need anything. Take Onesimus here, he is fleet of foot and knows the way like the back of his hand." Giving Nicanor a quick hug, she said, "I thank the Lord you have returned. We need you at times like this."

There it was again, that talk about not a lord, but "the Lord." Nicanor didn't know what to think. How could she be so confident there was only one? But that was a subject for another day. Time was wasting. It was already the third hour of the night. The party of five, with Onesimus leading the way, headed out with cloaks pulled over their heads, leaning into the wind and heading uphill, their sandals slipping on the wet and stony path. This was no night to be out in the dark, but there was no choice. Something had gone awry.

Even in broad daylight the journey up the hill to the back side of the Acro-Corinth would have taken at least an hour at a quick pace. As it was, this journey might take twice that amount of time, for there were several splits in the trail. One had to choose the right path three different times to get to where the aqueduct channel branched off from the main aqueduct and headed down the hill toward Erastos's villa. There were only fields and rock walls along this path, and nothing to light the way except the small hand lamps that each of them carried. About thirty minutes into the hike, with the rain picking up, Onesimus's lamp sputtered and went out. With Malchus's help, he dried his wick, checked the oil and relit his lamp. But precious moments had been lost. Everyone in the party had a sense of urgency, and the anxiety in their faces was visible in the flickering flames of the lamps.

After still another thirty minutes, and with the rain now pelting down, the soaked travelers reached the spot where the path angled almost directly uphill, up the side of the Acro-Corinth, arcing to the left gradually to the aqueduct. With water dripping off his nose, Onesimus turned to Nicanor and said, "We should have seen some light by now, if he is still up here. And where is his horse? He rode out this morning on his horse." Only a split second later they heard a muffled whinny, off to the left in the distance, perhaps ten *stadia* away.[1]

"Over there!" shouted Onesmius. "That must be Bucephalus!" As they hurried in the direction of the sound, Onesimus raised his strong voice and shouted into the rain, "We are coming, boy. We are coming, Bucephalus!" It took another fifteen minutes, with Onesimus running pell-mell across the slope toward the aqueduct, before they reached the horse. There he stood, soaking wet in the cold winter rain. Nicanor's cloak was soaked through and felt like it weighed as much as a horse's saddle. Out of breath, he came up beside the horse, and whispered in his ear, "Where is he, old friend? Where is he?" Nicanor had often ridden this horse on errands for Erastos, and Bucephalus knew him in an instant. Bucephalus restlessly pawed the ground.

"Erastos must be nearby. Bucephalus knows the way home, and would have found his way if the master had sent him home on his own," said Onesimus somewhat hopefully.

Again, Nicanor spoke gently to the horse, stroking his mane. "Where is he, old boy? Lead me to him." Slowly, deliberately, the horse walked up the path. Even in the rain, the enormous, dark form of the aqueduct was visible, towering some two or three stories up to the top channel. The horse passed under the arch of the aqueduct to the other side, where the smaller side channel shunted off to the left. There, right at the split, was a form on the ground. Bucephalus went over and nudged it, but

---

[1] A *stadia*, from which we get the word *stadium*, was a standard length of distance especially used in Olympic-style games. It was about 607 feet in length. Ten stadia then would be just over a mile.

there was no movement. "Bring me more light, quickly, and Xerxes, come up here." Shining all the available light on the dark form, their deepest fears were realized. There was Erastos, prone, motionless, with a bloody lump on the back of his head. It looked as if he had been struck from behind by a rock or other hard object. Crouching down on his hands and knees, Xerxes placed his ear on Erastos's chest. "There is still breath in him, but very shallow. We must get him home as quickly as possible so we can deal with his wound."

Nicanor, taking charge, said, "Onesimus, run as quickly as you can back home. Tell Lady Camilla we have found him, he is alive, and we are coming. Tell her only that he is hurt, and to prepare to receive him—dry clothes, a dry bed, some compresses, a bowl of clean water, some bandages. Can you remember all of that?"

"Yes, Master. I can, and I am off," said Onesimus as he disappeared into the night.

"Here is what we must do," said Nicanor. "Xerxes, we must get the master on the horse, with me holding him. And since you are small, you can sit in front of Erastos, so we can brace him on both sides. I will strap him to myself with this cord around our two waists. Malchus, you and the other servants, spend a little time looking around to see if you can see what may have happened here. But make it brief. We will ride straight back to the villa."

Bucephalus, like Alexander's horse for which he was named, was a large white stallion, perhaps nineteen hands high, and he could easily carry the weight of the three men. With Malchus holding the horse's reins, Nicanor climbed onto the back end of the horse. When the servants had carefully lifted Erastos up into the saddle, Nicanor put his arms around him to hold him upright. Finally, Xerxes stepped high up into the stirrup of the horse and slid in front of Erastos. Xerxes took the reins and they headed down the hill to the villa. Nicanor, with his head pressed against Erastos's back, could barely hear his breathing and the ominous sound of a rattle in his chest.

8

THE PROPOSITION

♦ ♦ ♦

There was little sleeping that night, and by morning Nicanor was lingering outside the room where Erastos was lying unconscious, with his head bandaged. Erastos's breathing sounded normal—in fact, he seemed to be sleeping. And little Julia had refused to leave her father's side. She was cuddled up next to him on the bed, holding his hand and saying little prayers when she awoke. Outside the rain continued, and the little brazier warming Erastos's room was the sole defense against the damp and gloom.

The ever-sensible Camilla had had enough of Nicanor's pacing and hovering.

"Now, shoo . . . Nicanor! Two fretting women in this room is more than enough to watch over Erastos. Xerxes says he is in no further danger at the moment, and we will be saying our prayers to the Lord Jesus. Besides, you haven't even had a chance to visit your shop on the Lechaion Road. I'll bet Gordianus is wondering if you will ever reappear. You need to tend to your own affairs."

Reluctantly Nicanor put on his warmest, most weather-proof cloak, and headed out into the rain. However you looked at it, this did not augur well for the future, as Nicanor valued Erastos's friendship and advice and even his tutelage in business. He ought to say a prayer as well for Erastos, but to which god? He wasn't sure. Maybe Asclepius the healer. "I certainly hope Xerxes is right and knows what he is doing." Nicanor did not have complete trust in the doctors and was very skeptical of miracles.

♦ A CLOSER LOOK ♦

Hippocrates and
Ancient Greek Medicine

Long before the second century A.D., when the famous Roman Galen wrote his treatises on medicine and anatomy, the long legacy of Hippocrates had had its effect. Born around 460 B.C. on the island of Cos during the golden age of Greece, Hippocrates is known today as the father of modern clinical medicine, and the modern medical Hippocratic Oath is named after him.

Hippocrates is thought to be the first to conclude that diseases were due to natural causes and were not to be attributed to deities or other superstitious causes. Hippocrates was said, by the disciples of Pythagoras, to be the one who linked philosophy with medicine while separating religion from the discipline of medicine. It is difficult for us to imagine today the breakthrough in viewing disease as a result of factors such as diet, living habits and environment. But this was Hippocrates's achievement: he does not attribute a single illness to a spiritual cause. At the same time, however, he drew numerous erroneous deductions about human anatomy and related matters. A famous example is the idea that bodily "humors," the interaction of fluids in the body (blood, phlegm, black and yellow bile) may explain health and illness.

Hippocrates believed in taking a passive approach to treatment. He affirmed "the healing power of nature." In other words, the body has within itself the power to heal itself, in part by rebalancing the four humors in the body. Thus Hippocratic therapy concentrated on facilitating this natural process, and so rest and immobilization were of paramount importance. In the case of an injury, such as Erastos has in our story, the prescription was exactly the same—rest and immobilization. Hippocratic treatment was gentle, not drastic, stressing that one had to keep the patient clean and sterile, using only clean water or wine on wounds, though Hippocrates preferred a dry treatment, such as a soothing balm.

While reluctant to resort to drugs, occasionally Hippocrates would use potent medicine. The passive approach worked well with things like wounds or broken bones. But because the theory and practice of medicine was in its infancy, physicians sometimes could do no more than rely on their keen powers of observation and their knowledge of data collected from similar cases. Nevertheless, ancient physicians did practice surgery at a surprisingly sophisticated level, such as the mending of bones and wounds, and even certain types of internal surgery.

Since Nicanor had not had time to clean up properly after rescuing Erastos, he decided to go to the baths before visiting his shop. Once on the edge of the old city, Nicanor turned south for a few stadia to reach the better of the two baths in Corinth. He knew some of the slaves who worked there, and it would be good not only to bathe, but have a good shave.

Clean and refreshed, Nicanor walked the fifteen minutes down to his shop. Seeing the sign with the Corinthian column on it, he smiled. Despite the events of the last twenty-four hours,

♦ A CLOSER LOOK ♦

The Baths, Part Two

Figure 8.1. A man sitting in the frigidarium

In a prosperous city like first-century Corinth, the bath complexes could be elaborate and even served as a status symbol of a city on the rise (like sports complexes in American cities today). But once one emerged from the bathing process, one was far from done. There were slaves there to help the visitors complete the grooming process.

One of the regular practices at the baths was the scraping of dirt and sweat from the skin using an instrument called a *strigil*, a small curved knife (see figure 8.2 below). Soaps, while known in the ancient world (Celts were known to use balls of an alkaline substance) had not been adopted in Roman society. Instead, perfumed oil was applied to the skin and then scraped off along with the dirt. People of means would assign this task to their slaves. Strigils came in different sizes for different parts of the body. Believe it or not, star gladiators were known to have their sweat scraped off, collected in small bottles and sold to their fans!

The laundry too might be part of this complex. It would be situated right next to the toilets, for the ancients had discovered that human urine was one of the best bleaching agents for whitening a toga and making it look new again. And here was yet another reason for using perfumed oil on the scalp and elsewhere in the final stage of grooming, for even with a thorough rinsing the bleached toga could still carry an odor. Romans, unlike Greeks, usually preferred the clean-shaven look, and indeed they used "hair-pluckers" and depilatories to make their arms and legs look clean and smooth.

Figure 8.2. A strigil

it was good to be home and back tending to his own business. The door of the shop stood ajar and Nicanor could hear the dull thudding of metal on stone from inside. The job of repairing the main aqueduct was taking longer than expected. The initial survey of the job had taken place under Nicanor's supervision just before he embarked for Roma. New leaks had been discovered as the work progressed. The repair entailed a lot of cutting of new stone and chiseling old stone. It also called for turning off the water for a period of time to do the repairs. But at this juncture only the preparatory stone cutting was in process.

Gordianus was no ordinary man. At a glance you might think he was a gladiator, or perhaps the bouncer at a taberna. In fact, this giant hulk of a man was a sweet, gentle soul, with an artistic side. While he was working in stone to feed his family, sculpting was his passion. He was gregarious, friendly and wouldn't harm a fly, at least not knowingly or willingly. Standing a good six feet five inches tall and weighing close to 250 pounds, he took up much of the space in the little shop on the Lechaion Road owned by Nicanor.

"Hey, Tiny," yelled Nicanor as he came through the door. "Well met after so long."

"Tiny" came over and gave Nicanor such a crushing bear hug that his ribs ached.

"Alright, alright, enough!" Nicanor protested.

"Welcome home, boss."

"Don't call me boss." Nicanor smiled. "We work together. Where do we stand with the goal of having enough stone cut to cart it up the hill and do the repairs?"

"It's going to take a bit more time. And we will have to hire a sledge and some slaves to drag the stone up to the aqueduct. Even I cannot cart all this stone very far. And I have to tell you something strange."

"Yes?" prompted Nicanor, looking quizzical.

"When I was up at the aqueduct two days ago taking measurements, I noticed two odd things. First of all, someone had deliberately put a large boulder in the shunt line that flows down the hill to Erastos's land. That rock could never have found its way there accidentally. Naturally enough, I took a pole and pried it out. That took no little time. But I figured Erastos would then owe you one."

"And what was the second thing?"

"This was even stranger. Early in the day, before it started to rain, I saw a couple of heavies wandering around aimlessly near the shunt line from the aqueduct. Not doing anything . . . they were just sitting or walking around. I thought it was odd but none of my business, so I continued on around the hill to the spot where we will make the repairs. But later, as I hurried down the hill in the rain, I noticed a large white horse standing alone in the distance under an olive tree. I figured it had run away. But I didn't stop since my wife would already be angry because I was late for supper."

Nicanor looked down at the shop floor pensively and stood silent for a minute. He turned around and looked out at the road, where the rain-washed stones gleamed in the morning sun. Turning back around he said, "Well, I was not going to trouble you with this, but last night we found Erastos up there near the horse, unconscious, lying on the ground with a huge lump on his head. I'm afraid this looks like foul play now, not a mere accidental fall."

"That does not augur well for Erastos. And who would want to do him harm anyway? He is a noble and honest soul."

"Well, I can think of one person, who shall remain nameless for the moment," said Nicanor.

As if on cue, there came a knock on the door. Answering it, Nicanor found Publius, Aemilianus's head servant, standing there with a grin on his face.

"Master Nicanor, a word in private please," said Publius, beckoning Nicanor with the motion of his finger.

Nicanor stepped outside the shop and Publius then whispered, "My master has sent me to retrieve you at once. He has something urgent to say to you, I do not know what. But he asks that you please meet him shortly down near the *odeon* at the Castor and Pollux *caupona*. In the back room. He says it is an urgent business matter."

"I'll bet it is," said Nicanor with a premonition of dread.

"Okay, I will come now." Waving at Gordianus, he said, "Back shortly."

The Castor and Pollux, as cauponae went, was more upscale than most such drinking establishments. Situated on the top of the hill overlooking the odeon, out beyond the spreading olive groves and vineyards one could even see the blue water of the Adriatic in the distance. The large wooden sign that hung over the door of the establishment showed the twin brothers Castor and Pollux, freshly painted in bright colors and surrounded by a background of stars against a night sky. This sign could be seen all the way from the sea road below, several stadia away. As always, the key to its success was location, location, location.

◆ A CLOSER LOOK ◆

Wining and Dining
in Roman Corinth

Dining in a Roman colony city took place in a variety of venues. For those not very well off, those not invited to dinner parties in temple dining rooms or fancy villas, there were three choices— the popina, the caupona or the taberna. The popina was the ancient equivalent of a fast-food restaurant. It was often built right into the front of a house and had a marble bar into which had been carved holes big enough to hold large clay pots of soup or other warm food that one could consume on the street or on the run. A caupona, however, provided full-service meals and drinks and had rooms for meetings. In either a caupona or a taberna one was likely to find all sorts of people from all walks in life—sailors, butchers, coffin makers, stone masons, eunuchs, priests and businessmen making deals.

The general impression from the literature is that a taberna tended to be the low end of the spectrum and the caupona a bit more up-scale. A person of patrician blood might well meet a freedman like Nicanor in a caupona, but he would not normally stoop to going to a taberna. That same patrician wouldn't think of inviting a freedman to a dinner party in a temple or in his home, unless he had already become part of his extended family or network of regular clients.

The Emperors Tiberius and Claudius had both placed restrictions on tabernae and cauponae, seeing them as breeding grounds for various sorts of troublemaking. In fact Claudius had recently banned the selling of meat in such establishments, to the resounding protest of the owners of such shops in Corinth. The real difference between the particular caupona of our narrative and some nearby tabernae was that there were no ladies of the night housed upstairs. And this caupona had a good reputation for being clean and not watering down its wine too much.

Publius led Nicanor directly past the bar, waving at the bartender, and into the back room lodged at the far right back corner of the establishment. Aemilianus was already there drinking some wine, and as he saw Nicanor come through the door, he poured another cup and rose to greet Nicanor.

"Vale, Nicanor! Welcome home. I trust the sea voyage went well."

"Actually, the passage was rough, but I managed to survive. It is good to be back on terra firma again."

"Indeed. Have a seat, as I have a proposition for you. Even larger than the last one. I am prepared to make you an offer I trust you can't refuse."

Sitting down on a small wooden stool, Nicanor got the sense

that this might be a day that would change his life forever. But as savvy as he was, even he had not anticipated what Aemilianus would say next.

Looking a bit disconsolate, and trying to appear a sympathetic figure, Aemilianus cleared his throat and began. "As you know, the gods have not favored my wife and me with a son, and I am of an age now that I must think about the future more clearly and plan more carefully. I have concluded that the best way forward is to adopt a son and make him my heir." With this he paused for effect and took another drink.

Nicanor figured he was supposed to say something, so he remarked, "A wise move, sir, and it will give you someone to pass your business to in the future. You will be able to rest assured that your legacy and name will go on. May the gods bless you as you make your choice."

A grin crossed Aemilianus's face, and he said, "Oh, I have already made my choice."

"Excellent," said Nicanor. "And may I ask who it will be?"

"*You!*" said Aemilianus in a strong voice. "I wish to make you my son and heir. I think you are the perfect choice, and one that will not require a lot of instruction or preparation."

Nicanor had not expected this. Indeed, when Aemilianus made his pronouncement, Nicanor had choked on his wine, spitting some of it on the table. A coughing fit followed, which compelled Publius, standing on guard in the doorway, to come over and pound Nicanor on the back.

"You are clearly surprised." Aemilianus smiled. "I hope you are also pleased and will feel compelled to say yes."

Nicanor felt like a great iron band was tightening around his head. How could he refuse such a magnanimous offer without becoming Public Enemy Number One of Aemilianus for the rest of his days? Desperate thoughts raced through his brain. He might have to flee from Corinth to escape Aemilianus and his hit men. *Think, Nicanor.* His mind raced. *Think how you can stall for time.*

Nicanor cleared his throat, and with every bit of sincerity he could muster, said in a quiet voice, "You overwhelm me with your generosity, my lord. I had thought this would merely be a meeting about what we had previously discussed concerning Erastos. But this new offer, I could never have imagined it in a thousand years. My lord, as you know I have just returned home, with many demands on me, catching up with things. As you may or may not know, Erastos has met with some kind of accident, and I have promised Camilla I will stand by her and help."

At the mention of Erastos, Aemilanus did his best not to grind his teeth. Instead he feigned shock and asked, "Is Erastos not well, then? I am sorry to hear this."

"No, my lord, he is not well. Hopefully even now he is recovering from an injury to his head. We should pray that Asclepius will help him. But in any case, I must ask you for the small kindness and understanding to give me a few days to get my affairs in order, fulfill my promises to Camilla and then get back to you. I will not keep you waiting for long, as I know how important this is to you, and what an honor it would be for me. But I must clear my mind and even pray about it."

Aemilianus was quiet for a moment, and then thought it wise to say, "Alright, but I will ask you to get back to me no later than Sunday next, the evening of the Ides of Februarius."

Swallowing hard and extending his hand, Nicanor concluded by saying, "You have my word on it. I will get back to you before cock crow, on the day of the sun." But as he left the caupona he muttered to himself, "Now I am truly trapped. What have I gotten myself into?"

9

THE TRIAL OF PAULOS

♦ ♦ ♦

Long before the sun showed its head above the horizon, Paulos was already up and busy. He had said his morning prayers, eaten breakfast and was preparing for the company that would be arriving shortly. With Camilla's permission he had acquired the valuable services of Tertius, the scribe who was in the employ of Erastos, as he had a letter he needed to write to his converts in Thessalonike. He had not heard from them or from Timothy or Silas in a while. And he was concerned that the situation, which had previously involved severe persecution and even the death of several converts, had worsened. No news could only mean bad news, in Paulos's way of thinking. Besides all this, his trial, which normally would have begun at dawn, had been postponed by Gallio until midday because of urgent business brought to him by an embassy from Athens the day before. While the trial weighed heavily on Paulos's mind, he did not want to waste time. So he had asked Tertius to come at dawn to take dictation of this letter.

Tertius was a slender man with long fingers, a good attribute for a scribe who had to use a stylus day after day. While Tertius was no Tiro, the famous scribe of Cicero who had invented *tachygraphy*, the art of shorthand, nevertheless Tertius was a steady and reliable secretary with a fine and very readable hand. Paulos had no reason to complain about his skills, but dictation would take a little longer with him than with the more elite scribes of the Greco-Roman world.

The knock came on the door just as a little light began to peek through the window in the front room of the house Paulos shared with Priscilla and Aquila. The apostle had been very quiet as he did not want to disturb Priscilla, who was still sleeping in the back of the house. Quietly opening the door, Paulos greeted Tertius and whispered to him that they should go and sit on the bench in the garden. Though it was a little chilly, the garden would be fine as a place for dictation, which could be a noisy activity.

Sitting on the stone bench facing Paulos, Tertius opened his wax tablet, took out his stylus from its small metal container and said, "I am ready, sir, when you are."

The procedure was reasonably simple. Tertius was to take down the letter on the *diptych* before him, then he would return to the house of Erastos and make two fair hand copies of the letter in *scriptum continuum*, a continuous flow of letters with little or no break or punctuation. But before the second copy was made, Paulos would need to review the first one to make sure all was right. Papyrus, ink and styli were not cheap and neither Paulos nor Tertius could afford to waste materials that were rather expensive. Once the document was to Paulos's satisfaction, he would have to find someone to take it to Thessalonike. If only he had remembered earlier that Aquila was going that way! In any case Paulos preferred to have coworkers deliver his letters so they could read them aloud and maximize their rhetorical effect.

Clearing his throat Paulos began: "Paulos, Silas and Timothy,

"To the church of the Thessalonians in God our Father and the Lord Jesus Christ:

"Grace and peace to you from God the Father and the Lord Jesus Christ.

"We ought always to thank God for you, brothers and sisters, and rightly so, because your faith is growing more and more, and the love all of you have for one another is increasing. Therefore, among God's churches we boast about your perseverance and faith in all the persecutions and trials you are enduring.

"All this is evidence that God's judgment is right, and as a result you will be counted worthy of the kingdom of God, for which you are suffering. God is just: he will pay back trouble to those who trouble you and give relief to you who are troubled, and to us as well. This will happen when the Lord Jesus is revealed from heaven in blazing fire with his powerful angels. He will punish those who do not know God and do not obey the gospel of our Lord Jesus. They will be punished with everlasting destruction and shut out from the presence of the Lord and from the glory of his might on the day he comes to be glorified in his holy people and to be marveled at among all those who have believed. This includes you, because you believed our testimony to you.

"With this in mind, we constantly pray for you, that our God may make you worthy of his calling, and that by his power he may bring to fruition your every desire for goodness and your every deed prompted by faith. We pray this so that the name of our Lord Jesus may be glorified in you, and you in him, according to the grace of our God and the Lord Jesus Christ."

Paulos was nowhere near through with this rhetorical discourse, but it had already taken some thirty minutes just to dictate this much of the document. He had to stop after every sentence for Tertius to catch up, and almost one whole side of the tablet was already filled with Greek capital letters. The apostle's plan was to wait until Silas or Timothy showed up, let them read and comment on it and then send one of them back to Thessalonike to deliver and interpret it.

Just then Priscilla walked into the garden carrying a tray with bread, olives, dried fish and wine so they could have a bit of a meal while they worked. "You remember you need to leave for the bema a little before the sixth hour," said Priscilla in a gentle voice.

Looking at the sundial in the garden Paulos replied, "And it is time now for me to freshen up and put on my best toga for this occasion. And I must find the little diptych with my Roman citizenship authentication. Tertius, we will finish this perhaps tomorrow, but you can make a start on the first fair hand copy while I am occupied with dealing with this little legal matter that confronts me today."

"Very good, sir, and may God be with you and vindicate you, if you don't mind my saying so."

Figure 9.1. Synagogue Lintel (stone)

"No, indeed, and please say a prayer for me that all will go well, for the remaining synagogue leaders are very angry with me."

◆ A CLOSER LOOK ◆

Jews in Corinth

There had been for a long time a sizable Jewish population in Corinth. The Jewish writer Philo, already in the 40s, said there was a considerable Jewish community in Corinth (*Leg. Ad Gaius*, 281-82). As many as two-thirds of all Jews in Paul's day lived outside of Judea and Galilee, and they were found in most of the major cities in the Empire, making up about 7 percent of the total population of the Empire.

In Corinth they did business with everyone, but few of them socialized with Greeks and Romans who did not attend the synagogue in Corinth. They mostly kept to themselves. Many of them had ancestors who had been brought to Corinth as slaves to work at rebuilding the town in the time of Caesar, and to work in other similar trades. Now a considerable number of them were freedmen, and some of them were quite prosperous businessmen. And so a "synagogue of the Hebrews" had been built. Their occupations ranged from ship owners to ship workers, to artisans like Paul to merchants to slaves, to Roman citizens, and they ranged from very Hellenized to very traditionally Jewish, with only a precious few of them Roman citizens like Paul.

Jewish life centered around the synagogue in Corinth, and Crispus, the *archisynagogos*, or "ruler of the synagogue," who presided over its services, had been converted by Paul to his sectarian messianic Jewish religion over a year before our story takes place. As if it were not bad enough that one synagogue ruler had been converted, there were other synagogue members who defected as well, most recently Stephanus and his family. And this was the straw that broke the camel's back. When Stephanus and his family left and were baptized by Paul, the remaining synagogue leader, Sosthenes, resolved to take action against Paul, for the synagogue could not stand to lose any more high-status, well-educated patrons. Filing a complaint in the local basilica against Paul, the matter had finally come to the attention of Gallio, the proconsul, and the wheels of Roman justice had been set in motion.

The life of a Jewish evangelist like Paulos was precarious, especially when his own people largely rejected his message. In many ways he realized he was a man without an earthly country. Unwelcome in Judaea, and beaten, jailed or cast out of one town after another, the fact that he had been able to stay in Corinth for over a year without real trouble was something of a record respite. In part this was because he had a valuable trade to offer the town, and in part it was because he had converted enough high-status citizens that they had his back when necessary.

On this day, Paulos was feeling rather vulnerable when it came to friends and social protection. Where was Erastos or others who might come to his defense? On this morning they were nowhere to be found, and neither Crispus nor Stephanos showed up for the first appearance before Gallio. *Perhaps,* mused Paulos, *they have more confidence than I do about the outcome. Or perhaps they have simply taken my previous advice to be in prayer about this matter.* Whatever the case, Paulos would walk alone the one *stadium* from his shop down to the tribunal and bema, which was situated right on the Lechaion Road in the middle of the old town.

With his toga and appearance properly inspected by Priscilla, Paulos headed off to the center of town where the raised platform called the bema stood. "Maybe I will just get away

♦ A CLOSER LOOK ♦

Roman Jurisprudence

This episode in Paul's life can be rather precisely dated, as Gallio was only in Corinth for a couple of years before his health caused him to withdraw. He seems to have arrived in Corinth no later than May of A.D. 51, and we know he was gone by A.D. 53. Therefore, this trial probably occurred about A.D. 52.

The process of a Roman trial in the provinces was clear enough in Paul's day. The prosecution or plaintiff came before the proconsul and reported its case. The accused was then summoned to appear before the proconsul. In our story, both of these things have already happened. On occasion there would be a sort of preliminary fact-finding hearing, with the trial deferred until later while the judge mulled things over. Roman trials like these were trials by judge rather than trials by jury. Since, however, the trial proceedings in this case were accusatorial (that is, an accusation had already been leveled against Paul) rather than a matter of inquisition, Roman law required that the accusers had to appear with the defendant before the judge, and make their accusations directly. Once the accusations had been laid out in court, then the defendant himself must respond. In such trials the legal rule was that the burden of proof lay on the accuser. The judge had flexibility in establishing what the real bone of contention was and in determining the punishment.

We must assume that the case described in Acts 18 is an *extra ordinem* case, which required the governor or proconsul himself to hear and decide the matter. In Corinth this involved the proconsul coming and sitting on the tribunal on a judgment seat, or bema, and personally deciding the matter. He would be assisted by his advisory council and his *notarius*, who wrote up the minutes of the proceedings. While the proconsul could render summary justice by immediately deciding the issue, he could also postpone rendering a verdict and neither party in the litigation could speed up the process. Indeed the proconsul could postpone things indefinitely because he had *imperium*, the authority and power and authorization from the Senate to do what he thought best for all concerned, and especially for Rome. Postponements could be devastating. For example, the famous historian Polybius was under arrest for an incredible fifteen years "under suspicion" as he awaited the resolution of his trial.

with a fine this time, for being a nuisance," murmured Paulos to himself. The abuses and beatings had begun to take their toll on the apostle, and on this damp morning he felt discomfort in his joints as he walked along, trying to show his dignitas while at the same time knowing he was showing his age.

A breeze blew down the street, making Paulos shiver a bit, and the gray clouds scudded by overhead. But at least it wasn't raining. Up ahead Paulos could see the crowd gathering at the

Figure 9.2. The bema

bema, and behind him he suddenly heard a trumpet blast, signaling that the proconsul was on his way and warning those scurrying up and down the street to get out of the way of his entourage. Gallio rode in a horse-drawn carriage, which indicated his stature and status.

With help from his notarius, or recording secretary, Gallio climbed up onto the bema, with a slave carrying his *curule* chair. With the plaintiffs to his right and Paulos to his left, both standing below the elevated tribunal that stood some eight feet above street

Figure 9.3. A curule chair

level, a hush fell over the crowd. Gallio sorted out his toga. There was a *lictor* standing close by Gallio holding the *fasces*.

The traditional symbol of Roman authority was the fasces, a bundle of birch rods approximately five feet long tied together with a red leather ribbon to form a sort of cylinder. They symbolized a magistrate's power. Lictors would carry the fasces, accompanying the magistrates to wherever they were going to perform their official duty. The fasces could include an ax or two, with the blades sticking sideways out of the bundle. While the fasces traditionally represented the power of life or death (i.e., by beating with rods, or by decapitation), in the New Testament period no magistrate could execute a Roman citizen without a trial.

The fasces made clear that Roman justice would be done in this place on this day. Turning to Sosthenes, and the some ten men from the synagogue quorum standing by him, Gallio raised

Figure 9.4.
Roman fasces

his hand and simply said, "Proceed."

Sosthenes, a young man with a strong voice, began: "O noble proconsul, we come before you this day with a serious grievance against this man, Paulos, who has been disrupting our lawful assemblies in the synagogue here in Corinth. We, your peace-loving subjects, desire nothing so much as to be able to practice our own legal religion, which the Emperor Claudius has again affirmed our right to do. We are good residents of this town and we pay our taxes on time, and we only seek to live in peace with all our neighbors, be they Romans, Greeks or Jews. But this man Paulos has come into our place of worship and into our lives wreaking havoc, dividing parents from children, and husbands from wives, and even casting a spell over our former leader, Crispus, such that he was carried away in this superstition that Paulos preaches about a crucified savior named Christos."

At this Gallio grunted and nearly laughed, for the idea of a crucified savior or god seemed ridiculous to him, but he maintained his decorum.

"Noble Gallio, we would not trouble you with this matter except this man is persuading people to worship God in ways that are contrary to law—"

With this remark, which got at the heart of the matter, Gallio cut Sosthenes off. "I have heard enough. You say this

Paulos persuades people to worship your God in ways contrary to your law?"

"Yes, Your Honor," replied Sosthenes.

"What is that to me? Corinth is a city in which many gods, including yours, are worshiped in whatever way the local priests or leaders see fit. Your religion is a licit one, and you may practice it as you see fit within the bounds of Roman law, but unless this man, Paulos, can be shown to be guilty of violating Roman law, then this is most certainly a matter for you to attend to yourself, and not be troubling this court with it!" Toward the end of this outburst by Gallio, he was virtually shouting at the men standing below. "If it were a matter of a crime or serious villainy, I would be justified in accepting the complaint of you always-complaining Jews, but since it is just a matter about words and names and your own Jewish law, see to it yourselves. I do not wish to, indeed, I refuse to be the judge of such petty matters!" And with this he dismissed them all from the tribunal.

Almost immediately the men from the quorum seized Sosthenes and started beating him, saying, "We knew this would never work. And now you have irritated the proconsul and publicly shamed us before him, so we will now exact punishment, shaming you right here on the street!"

To this Gallio turned a blind eye, saying quietly to the notarius, "And thank you for informing me that this Paulos is a Roman citizen whose name has been recorded in the city census ledger for over a year. What fools these Jews were to try to prosecute him."

Paulos could hear all this going on behind his back. Wisely, having bowed in the direction of the proconsul, he had simply

♦ A CLOSER LOOK ♦

Roman Trials

At trials such as Paul's, the prosecution would often hire a rhetorically trained professional lawyer to argue their case. Apparently, however, Sosthenes did not have the funds, or did not think it necessary to do this. Rather, the Jewish community itself, led by him, made the accusations. This was a strategic mistake on several grounds. First, Paul had been through such trials before (e.g., in Philippi) and had been released. He knew what to expect. Second, Paul was a trained rhetorician, and no doubt he would come to court prepared to speak his *apologia*, his personal defense, using his best forensic rhetoric. Finally, Paul was also a Roman citizen, though Sosthenes might not have known this. So Paul had a trump card in his back pocket if he needed it. What Sosthenes had also apparently not taken into account was that Gallio had no patience with complaining Jews, especially when the complaint had to do with their own religion and a fellow Jew like Paul.

The accusation against Paul as recorded in Acts 18:13 is rather ambiguous, and perhaps deliberately so. Does it refer to the Jewish or Roman laws about worship and religion that Paul had offended? The context makes clear (noting the reference to "the God") that it is Jewish law he is said to be offending and Gallio's reaction makes this certain, for he says it is a matter for the Jews' internal community. The problem, of course, was that Rome reserved for itself the right of capital, and usually also corporal, punishment, especially of Roman citizens.

Could Sosthenes have been insinuating that Paul was preaching a new and illicit religion? This is certainly possible, and this is probably the accusation that landed Paul before the Areopagus in Athens. If they could have made the case to Gallio that what Paul was preaching was not a form of Judaism, he could have been in hot water. But Gallio does not think this is the case. As we see from the end of the story in Acts 18, Gallio does not see the actions of Paul as involving either a real crime or a serious fraud or deception, much less treason or *maiestas* of some sort. Rather, it is "a dispute about names and words and laws that (only) you observe." So it is that Gallio throws the ball back into Sosthenes's court saying, "Deal with this yourself, with a formal ruling; I do not wish to be the judge of this matter." As Roman legal experts have pointed out, this is precisely the correct answer of a Roman magistrate who is refusing to exercise his authority or power in an extra ordinem matter. We should not take this verdict to mean that Gallio was taking Paul's side; rather, he was saying it was an internal matter for the Jewish community to resolve.

Finally, there are three telling signs that Gallio had little sympathy for these Jewish plaintiffs. He addressed them as "O you Jews," which seems to reflect disdain. He refuses to act on their complaint, and finally, when he has them all cast out of the space before the bema, he turns a blind eye to the fact that Sosthenes is physically assaulted by his own people. Notice as well that Paul feels secure enough after this incident to stay in Corinth for a considerable time, of unspecified length, thereafter.[a]

---

[a]For much more on all this, and references to further reading, see my *The Acts of the Apostles* (Grand Rapids: Eerdmans, 1998), pp. 551-55 and the associated notes.

walked away from the bema. Perhaps someone like Erastos or Stephanos had already bent the ear of the notarius, without Paulos even knowing about it. A smile crept across his face and Paulos quoted the proverb to himself, "One who has unreliable friends soon comes to ruin, but there is a friend who sticks closer than a brother." Wait until he told Priscilla, still praying at the house, about how summarily and swiftly Roman justice worked!

10

JULIA'S PRAYERS AND NICANOR'S PROTECTION

◆ ◆ ◆

Dies *Veneris*, the day of Venus, dawned in Corinth. The week was beginning to draw to a close. And there was no sign that Erastos was going to wake up any time soon. He was beginning to lose weight, and the facial muscles in his pale face had started to sag. Julia had stayed by his side day and night, and Camilla had as well, hoping for improvement. Xerxes continued to counsel patience and rest. What more could he do? An injury took time to heal. It was not like a disease that might be treated.

By the time Nicanor arrived at the entrance to Erastos's villa, it was about the third hour of the morning. He had much on his mind. His stomach had churned all night, and he had gotten very little sleep. It showed in a slightly surly disposition, which he tried to suppress before entering. Camilla had not come to the door, but Tyche, the doorman, had let him right in as if he were still a member of the household. When Camilla saw him coming through the atrium, she came running and gave him the kiss of greeting. But Nicanor could not help but notice her reddened eyes and a tear trickling down her right cheek.

"How is it with him?" asked Nicanor, half-afraid to inquire.

"There is no improvement. At the same time, there is no sign of him getting dramatically worse. But he has begun to lose weight."

"May I see him?"

"Of course. I should warn you Julia is in there and she is pretty overwrought. Of course, she thinks the world of you."

"Well, the feeling is mutual," said Nicanor, managing a slight smile.

As he entered the bedroom, Julia sat up, as she had been lying next to her father. Then she unexpectedly said, "I have been praying. Nicanor, do you know my Lord Jesus? He is the great physician, even greater than Xerxes or Asclepius."

"No, Julia, I am afraid I am of a skeptical mind. I do not know your Jesus."

"But you need to know him. He is the only one who can help you with your problems, and he will help my pater as well!"

Nicanor was surprised by this remark and wondered if someone had been talking to Julia. "How do you know I have problems?"

"It is written all over your face. You are very worried about something, and not just about my pater either." Then, in her little seven-year-old voice, she asked, "Will you let me pray for you?"

Nicanor could hardly say no to this, so he just nodded.

"Take my hand then, and let us pray." Julia's hand disappeared into Nicanor's much larger hand. "Dear Lord Jesus, you know all things. You know what is on my teacher's heart and what he wants and needs. You also know my pater needs you now, needs healing. Could you please fix these two problems? I know you know what is best, and your timing is always right, so I will just leave these requests in your hands. Bless Nicanor, and help him know what he must do or decide. Amen."

Nicanor was touched by the sincerity of Julia and the earnestness of her prayer. His heart ached because he knew he did not have the trust in the divine that she so evidently had. He envied her simplicity and purity of heart. "Thank you so much. I am feeling a bit better now, as if a weight has been lifted. You keep praying for us. Someone is listening." Julia gave Nicanor a hug and said, "Please visit again soon. Why not come on the Lord's Day, the Day of the Sun? There will be many friends here then."

Nicanor winked at her and said, "I will think about it."

Seeing Camilla standing in the door, Nicanor rose and walked with her back toward the atrium.

"Camilla, I may know something about what happened to Erastos. My coworker Gordianus the Giant was up at the aqueduct, and he said he had seen some big men near the place where the channel splits off from the main aqueduct. Later he discovered a boulder lodged in the aqueduct and extracted it, which is why you have water flowing once again. And then later that day, in the evening when the rain had begun, he was heading home, down the hill, when he saw Bucephalus standing alone under an olive tree."

"So you think perhaps Erastos was a victim of foul play rather than a fall from his horse?"

"Yes, I do, and my question is, who are Erastos's enemies? Who would want to do him harm?"

"Honestly, he is so friendly and well liked, I would hesitate to say he has any enemies. He does have a competitor for the office of aedile, but surely that can have nothing to do with this, can it?"

♦ A CLOSER LOOK ♦

The Office of Aedile

The office of aedile had existed since the time of the early Republic, and was just below the office of *duovir* in the *cursus honorum*. It appears likely that the Greek terms *oikonomos* and *agoranomos*, the former of which we find used of Erastos in Romans 16:23, are the equivalents of the Latin term *aedile*. Among the main duties of the aedile was *cura urbis*, the maintaining of streets, marketplaces, public buildings and water systems, as well as collecting the rent from the publicly owned shops in town. We may speculate that this is how Paul met Erastos in the first place. Aediles in some places were also in charge of the Olympic-style games, which may have been another reason Erastos would have contact with Paul, because Paul was making a needed commodity, tents.

In addition, aediles had some responsibility for maintaining public order. Two aediles were selected from among the plebians, and two called *aediles curules* were selected from either the patricians or the plebians, but normally from the former. These served in effect as magistrates. The term *aedile* comes from the Latin *aedilis*, from *aedes* or *aedis*, a temple or consecrated building. The reason they would be in charge of festivals and games is that almost all such festivals and games were religious in character, sponsored by or celebrating one deity or another, and it appears that originally aediles were in charge of the upkeep of the temples. Needless to say, such festivals and games brought in major revenue for the city and for the temples.

"I don't know, but the thought did occur to me that if Erastos was incapacitated, Aemilianus would have a clear path to the position and the power it brings. We are not talking about just any kind of aedile, but a curule aedile, an aedile with great power, including being in charge of public works and being the city treasurer as well. A man who was hungry for power in Corinth could do a lot to establish his name and honor in that office."

Having said what he had come to say to Camilla, Nicanor excused himself, saying he needed to go see another possible employee for his business. Camilla waved as he headed back down the path toward Corinth, but this time he would take another route and head over to the school of the gladiators that stood between Corinth and Isthmia. It was time to find and talk to Krackus in earnest. Nicanor was pretty sure he needed to muscle up about now.

The school of the gladiators was a noisy place, where slaves and freedmen honed their skills.

Figure 10.1. School of the gladiators in Pompeii

The large field surrounded by walls was a practice field for all the sorts of contests the gladiators would undertake in the arena. At the back of the complex were changing rooms, baths and even an infirmary. Having looked all over the field, and asked twice where Krackus was, Nicanor finally found him in the infirmary getting his bulging right bicep stitched up. Nicanor stepped into the room quietly and saw Krackus wince again and then again and again, as the doctor sewed him up. Finally the huge man looked up, saw Nicanor and smiled.

"Vale, Nicanor. What brings you to my neighborhood?"

"We'll get to that in a moment, but the better question is, what happened to you? I thought you practiced with wooden swords and the like."

Krackus chuckled and said, "Well . . . we usually do, but we have this young up-and-coming gladiator named Stephanus who was dying to get a chance to actually test my skills, and you know how it is with gladiators. It would besmirch their honor if they backed down from a challenge like that, even a friendly one. So, anyway, we were going at it in the back of the field over there, when I was suddenly distracted. Some women were standing on the hill looking over the wall, and one of them yelled, 'Oh Krackus, if only you would be mine!' I turned my head for just an instant, and *whack!* Young Stephanus stabbed me right in the upper arm. There used to be a day when I would never be distracted in the middle of a fight. I was so focused then! But now, more and more, I just can't seem to concentrate as well."

"Perhaps this is a word to you from Fortuna, this little flesh wound, because I have come here in earnest to offer you that job, starting immediately. With good pay and benefits. I need your help right now!"

Krackus stroked his lantern-like jaw for a minute or two, and then said, "I suppose it would be wise to get out while the getting is good."

"Exactly what I was just telling him, Master Nicanor," said the diminutive doctor as he finished up the last stitch.

There was more silence, and then a deep sigh. Krackus finally said, "Alright, I'll give it a try for a few weeks, and we'll see how it goes. I would like to finally be settled and have a home and family instead of constantly traveling all over Greece. And I reckon Corinth is as good a place to muster out of the gladiator trade as anywhere."

A big smile came across Nicanor's face. "You can't imagine how relieved I feel right now that you have said yes. I will wait for you to bathe and pack up your gear. Say your farewells to your employer and friends and we will head home."

"Sounds like a plan," said Krackus, and he leaped off the table then nearly crushed Nicanor's hand in his death grip of a handshake. *Maybe*, thought Nicanor, *I can now see a light at the end of the tunnel, and it won't be Aemilianus's thugs coming after me with their lanterns.*

11

THE INSULA AND
THE SABBATH

♦ ♦ ♦

Corinth was a city nowhere near the size of Roma with its teeming millions. On an average day in Februarius, when there were no festivals or games going on and no major ships in port, Corinth had about fifty thousand residents. Like all such cities, while about 2 to 5 percent of the population might be considered wealthy, 95 percent were not. In contrast to the palatial mansions or villas of the wealthy, most of the rest of the city dwellers lived in *insulae*, multi-level apartment complexes crammed together in several parts of town. In "that part of town," the streets were narrow, the sanitation deplorable (excrement was poured into the streets from chamber pots), and there were the usual social issues brought on by people living on top of one another, especially when the weather began to heat up. Among the insulae there were orphaned children running loose in the streets and old people sitting on street corners, sometimes begging. An average of 137 persons per acre, in these neighborhoods you were liable to see every imaginable form, shape and condition of humanity. And there was a wide variety of languages and accents, with Greek being the common denominator, not Latin.

The residents of the insulae in Corinth came from all over the Empire, not least because it was the crossroads of the Mediterranean and was the Empire's slave trade clearing-house. There were Egyptians, Parthians, Syrians, Jews, Asians, Greeks, Romans, Ethiopians and more, who had come into this double-port city from abroad and had never left because of work opportunities, especially in the building trade or in dockyard work in either of the two harbors.

The part of the neighborhood where Nicanor lived was a desirable section, favorably situated at the top of a hill where the wind usually blew downhill, away from his humble abode. Nicanor had gotten to know some of his neighbors, chiefly a one-armed Roman soldier named Cassius who had mustered out in Corinth. He had lost one of his arms at the battle of Philippi, when he fought for Octavian. He loved to tell war tales, especially when he was deep in his cups. Cassius lived two floors above Nicanor. But lately Nicanor had no time to sit around and listen to the tales and reminiscences of old soldiers.

The stench of the streets was not much of an issue for Nicanor except when the spring thermals blew up the hill from the Adriatic. His was a ground-level apartment, the most spacious of its sort. And he also owned the apartment immediately above the ground level, having bought both from the landlord at a time when the landlord had bet too much on a gladiator and lost.

The front wall next to the door of Nicanor's place was painted a bright red with a white stripe, and on the balcony a large bougainvillea vine produced crimson blooms in late spring and summer. He had even managed a little decorating, and he did what he could to keep his place clean and inviting, just in case Tyche favored him with a suitable wife. For now his apartment would be shared with Krackus, and so it would house two bachelors hoping to improve their lot in life.

As they walked down the Lechaion Road together, heading for the insulae, Nicanor decided to stop in his shop so Krackus could meet Gordianus, goliath to goliath. Gordianus was still chiseling away vigorously on a large block of limestone when the two men entered the shop's doorway.

"Vale, Gordianus. I have someone I'd like you to meet."

Gordianus looked up from the wooden bench on which he was sitting to see a familiar figure. "It's Krackus!" said Gordianus.

"Do I know you?" asked Krackus.

"No, no, why should you? I'm just a fan. I have gone to see you fight many times in Isthmia and elsewhere. My wife says you have helped us survive financially, as I keep betting on you."

Krackus laughed heartily, and said, "Well, you will have to find another favorite now. I am probably hanging up my sword and shield and coming to work for young Nicanor here, before I become another sad, broken-down old gladiator. At least I have resolved to give the life of a noncombatant a try for a few weeks."

"A wise move, no doubt, but I will be sad not to see you in the arena again. You're the best!" At that very moment, Nicanor had a bright idea. Two days hence, when he had to go give his answer to Aemilianus, he would take both these men with him for protection. He had still not fully decided what to do, but at the moment he was leaning toward turning the offer down, and he knew that would not be well received by Aemilianus. He

could not rid his mind of the suspicion that Aemilianus had
something to do with Erastos's injury. He had the motive, means
and opportunity to do Erastos harm. It was time to take Krackus
home, however, and let him unpack and get settled.

"Gordianus, I must help Krackus get settled in, but we will
reconnoiter in the morning. I have a favor to ask of you in regard
to the evening of the day of the sun, two days hence."

It was nearly sundown and the walk to the insula took
Nicanor and Krackus past the small synagogue. They stopped
for a minute to watch the Jews entering. "You may laugh at
this," said Krackus, "but I have always wondered what went on
in that little building once a week on this very day. I gather it's
some kind of worship service for their God?"

"That's right," said Nicanor, "and part of it is in a strange language too, the Hebrew language. There is singing in a minor mode,
and various kinds of prayers, and then there is a reading from a
sacred text. The Jews are odd in that, unlike we Greeks or Romans,
they have a holy book and they believe it is God-breathed, full of
prophecies and writing inspired by their God. Unlike us, who
might turn to a living sage or seer, or the oracle at Delphi up in the
mountains, they get their guidance for life from their holy book.
They call it 'Torah,' which I am told means 'instruction.' Here's
another interesting thing. Their women cannot be priestesses and
must always keep their heads covered. And the men also cover
their heads on their day of worship. It seems the Jews also have
their own calendar of feast and holy days, and they even reckon
the hours of the day from sundown to sundown, which is why
they are meeting this evening. For them, this evening, and all next
day until sundown, is their holy day, and they will not do any work
in the next twenty-four hours."

"Odd, very odd," said Krackus. "Who can believe in only one God? And how exactly do you know all this?"

"You forget I was once a tutor, and I had Jewish clients as well. They would welcome us into their worship service, but we would have to cover our heads. But we should save such adventures for another day. Let us go get you settled in your new residence."

"Will you be wanting me to start in your taberna tomorrow?"

"No, I want you to rest and heal up, and just accompany me. Learn some of my daily business, and watch my back." At this juncture Nicanor confided to Krackus the whole story about Aemilianus and his offer, and also his suspicions about what had happened to Erastos.

Krackus listened intently, and said, "This is a bad business, Master Nicanor. I have heard lots of bad things about Aemilianus. Did you know he once tried to rig a gladiatorial combat so he could make a fortune off his fellow bettors? He even approached me once with the proposition that he would pay me a king's ransom to lose a match. Of course, I shrugged him off and told him I would never do that. All that glitters is not gold, as the old proverb says. My honor was more important to me than money."

Nicanor thought about this, and nodded. Krackus might be a goliath, but he had a good head on his bulging shoulders.

The walk to the top of the hill overlooking the odeon was undertaken in silence, with both men lost in their thoughts. They reached the *insula* and all was quiet. "Let's have a decent meal together and a drink, and call it a day. Tomorrow is bound to be busy."

Krackus smiled and said, "I don't know how much sleep we will be getting if we turn in early, since there is apparently a play

Figure 11.1. A street in Pompeii. Note the chariot and cart runs in the street made of stone.

by Euripides on at the odeon below. I saw the playbill posted on a wall at the edge of the insulae. It said *The Bacchae* was to be performed. This can only mean lots of drinking and lots of bad singing and other sorts of noise well into the night."

Nicanor sighed and added, "So much for a little peace and quiet, but at least we can lock the door and lie still for a good number of hours. That should feel good." And with that the two men entered the house.

12

PAULOS, PRISCILLA
AND ERASTOS

◆ ◆ ◆

Paulos no longer regularly observed the Sabbath, except when he was in the company of Jews who did so, and so when the day of Saturn dawned, he could be found in the leather-working shop, sewing away on yet another tent. Priscilla was there as well, but Aquila was still on the road, probably heading home by way of Athens.

"Now that I have gotten beyond the debacle with Sosthenes, I'll never be welcome in that synagogue again. Their enmity toward me will be heartfelt, no doubt, but at least I will not be run out of town. There is more work to do for the Lord Jesus here, and we must be planning for the worship service in Erastos's home. I hear, though, that Erastos has had a fall and is not doing so well. Am I right?"

"You're right," said Priscilla. "I didn't want to trouble you with the matter while you faced the trial, but now that it's all over, we really must pay a visit and pray for the man."

"Yes, we must. He is the most important patron of our assembly, and we meet in his home. I hope Camilla will not think I have been avoiding them. It's just been a very tumultuous week. Perhaps Tertius has told her the news that things went well for me at the trial."

After another hour of working on the tents, Priscilla said, "Paulos, we should go now. The tents can wait, but Camilla and Erastos need our support and prayers."

"I'm bringing some anointing oil," said Paulos.

Paulos got up from his work stool, shook the leather scraps and shavings from his toga and put on his cloak. Then he and Priscilla headed toward the base of the Acro-Corinth, taking the right fork off the Lechaion Road as they passed the Fountain of Pirene.

You could smell the meat hanging under the arches of the arcade that surrounded the fountain. The city fathers had wisely channeled a stream not only to the fountain, but through the back part of the arcade so that a *macellum*, or meat market, could operate there in the shade of the arcade. The cool air rising up from the stream helped keep the meat from spoiling rapidly. Most of the meat had come from sacrifices in one or another of the temples in Corinth, and already a problem had begun to brew between the more high-status Gentile converts like Erastos, who saw no problem with dining in the temple of Asclepius and elsewhere, and those like the family of Crispus, who still observed Jewish customs and would not eat "meat offered to idols," even at a home like Erastos's. Paulos was going to have to give some instructions on these matters to the house churches in Corinth before it led to major divisions in the body of Christ. But today was not the day to act on this issue. Today was a day to pray for and lay hands on Erastos.

Things had been subdued and somber in the household of Erastos throughout the week, as there had been no sign of improvement at all in the condition of the master of the house. There had been an attempt on the previous day to get some warm soup into him, without success. He had simply choked, and the soup had dribbled out on his bed linens. Camilla, though she would not say this out loud and did her best not to show it, was becoming increasingly frantic. The Lord Jesus needed to do something, and in a hurry. There was hardly any muscle tone left in Erastos's limbs, and Xerxes had advised rolling him from one side to another during the day, to prevent bed sores on his backside.

Nicanor had promised Camilla he would check in again on Saturn's day, and so as he approached the villa of Erastos, it appeared to be mere coincidence that he arrived just as Paulos and Priscilla were going into the house, with Tyche holding the door for them. Waving at Tyche, Nicanor said, "Hold that door just a bit longer."

There was a subdued atmosphere in the house. The servants were tiptoeing around trying to be as quiet as possible. There was no weeping and wailing, but neither was there any laughter of children. Julia's older brothers had been sent away to their aunt Phoebe's house in nearby Cenchreae, the eastern port city of Corinth, as Phoebe was also a believer. Everyone who entered the house did so with a sense of foreboding.

Looking haggard and drawn, Camilla came out of the bedroom where Erastos still lay, and she tried to compose herself for her guest. When Paulos approached her, she gave him a hug and the kiss of greeting, then did the same for Priscilla and Nicanor.

♦ A CLOSER LOOK ♦

Greco-Roman Beliefs
About the Afterlife

Ancient pagan religion had little or nothing to do with attempts to obtain everlasting life, or to be "saved" in the Christian sense. The "salvation" most ancients were looking for was salvation from disease, disaster and death. The term *redemption* referred to a very mundane release from the bondage of slavery, not from the personal bondage of sin. When a slave went to a temple looking for "redemption," what he or she was looking for was manumission. When a petitioner went up the mountain to the oracle at Delphi, what they asked to be kept safe from were things like danger in travel, or danger in giving birth, or release from disease or debt or deliverance from a rival who was threatening them. In other words, "salvation" in the pagan mind almost always referred to something happening in this world, in this life, of direct material benefit. Even focusing on this life, as A. D. Nock showed long ago, most of the ancients didn't believe in the concept of "conversion," a radical transformation of human character. There could be healing, yes, perhaps by the god Asclepius, but after the healing, a person would still have the same character they always had and one day they would go on and die.

The Greek notion of the immortality of the soul, which only some affirmed, referred to the inherent immortality of a part of a human being. It was not a gift from God in midlife or at death. It had nothing to do with having a religious conversion. Yes, there was a belief in an underworld, where the shades of the departed resided. It was called Hades, and should not be confused with the Christian notion of hell.

It simply refers to the land of the dead. Charon took the coins off the deceased eyes, placed there by his loved ones to pay for the ferry ride down the river Styx or one of the other underground rivers into Hades, one of which was named Lethe. For a precious few, say a great military hero who died in battle, there was a belief that they might go not to just anywhere in Hades, but to the fields of Elysium, the nicest district of Hades, where the virtuous and pious and noble would reside forever.

"You can all come in at once, and then we must let him rest," said Camilla. "Xerxes can think of nothing better than a rest cure."

"I can think of something better," said Paulos, "and with your permission I am here not merely to pray but to anoint Erastos and lay hands on him for healing." Paulos had done what the Jews called "signs and wonders" before,[1] and clearly he was convinced that one was needed now, before Erastos slipped into the arms of Lethe.

Camilla nodded and could only say, "Yes, please," though secretly even she wondered if this could possibly help. Nicanor turned pale at the whole notion and saw in it something possibly very cruel if nothing good came of it. His skeptical heart was saying, *This man is a charlatan, preying on the desperate, and I'll bet a request for money comes next.* But that did not happen. Instead Paulos went directly to Erastos's bedside, and with a small vial of oil anointed the forehead of the pale, bedridden man with the slack jaw, and began to pray.

Priscilla stood behind Paulos, and laid her hand on his shoulder as if supporting him. He bent over Erastos and began to

---

[1]See Romans 15:18-19.

pray. "Dear Lord Jesus," he said, "the author and finisher of life, the great physician, the healer, the risen one who overcame the grave, I ask you now to please visit your servant Erastos. It was you who raised many who have already died and healed many who were deathly ill. We know that yours is the power, and it is not ours. But we ask that you come and minister to your good servant and devoted brother Erastos. His family needs him, his fellow Christians need him, I need him, Corinth needs him. Camilla and Julia have said many prayers, and we ask that you answer them now, in the presence of these witnesses, for we know that the truth of anything must be confirmed by the testimony of at least two witnesses, and we ask it in your precious name—risen Lord Jesus, Lord of all human life, amen."

What happened next caused goose bumps to rise on Nicanor's flesh. And indeed he was so shocked at what he saw that he began to shake all over. He had never seen, nor ever expected to see something like this, and his immediate impulse was a desire to flee the room, for he knew he was in the presence of something powerful and holy.

Erastos had nearly immediately opened his eyes and stared at Paulos. The color began to come back into his cheeks, and he struggled to sit up, with the help of Paulos. Camilla, holding on to Julia with a death grip, fell on her knees, looked up to the ceiling, and said, "All praise to the Lord Jesus, for he has seen the distress of his loved ones and heard their cries." And little Julia simply repeated those words as huge tears came rolling down her cheeks. She looked up at Nicanor, who had backed up against the wall to get as far away from the bed as possible, and asked him, "Do you want to know my Lord Jesus, now?" But Nicanor was stunned into silence. Priscilla began singing a *dox-*

ology, a glory word, to this God, and Camilla and the servants lurking at the door joined in.

Just then, Erastos opened his mouth and spoke. "What's all the fuss about? Haven't I just been sleeping? You'd think I had been dead. Why are you all standing or kneeling here as if you had just seen the shade of Julius Caesar himself? I am alive, and well, though I have to admit, I am starving . . ."

Camilla quickly clapped her hands and said, "Marcia, please, some soup and bread, and anything else the master wants." Meanwhile Paulos had stood up, a huge smile on his face, simply murmuring "*Soli deo gloria.*"

When Nicanor heard that, his first thought was, *Well, scratch the idea that he's a charlatan and a huckster.* He staggered out of the room in a daze trying to figure out what had just happened. He was trying to slink out the door quietly, when Camilla called to him and said, "You must stay for lunch and our celebration. Erastos no doubt will have much he wants to say to you."

"Yes, mistress," he replied, "but right now I am in need of a huge goblet of unwatered wine please." Tyche laughed and said, "Coming right up. But you have just drunk in the new wine of the gospel, of life and life abundant in the Lord Jesus, and that will help you much more." Just when Nicanor thought he was getting a handle on his new direction in life, then this had to happen! It seemed like he would have to do a lot more rethinking.

13

DIES SOLIS

The Morning of the Day of the Sun/Son

♦ ♦ ♦

At dawn on Dies Solis things in the household of Erastos had already gone into high gear. The master of the house was on the mend, and the household had a bounce back in its step. The servants were more cheerful, Camilla was in a better frame of mind, and little Julia was finally back to her old playful self. The meeting of the followers of Jesus would begin at the eleventh hour, or near sunset, just after all the workers and slaves were finished with work for the day. And there would be some from the other house churches who would arrive late to the meeting. Camilla was expecting as many as seventy this time, and was fretting about where many of them would eat, since the triclinium was not going to hold more than about twenty even if all the couches had several guests. She guessed some would have to stand in the atrium, but it might be chilly this Februrarius evening. For the moment at least, it was not raining. Indeed, old Sol was shining bright this morning, as if it too was celebrating the returning of Erastos to good health.

The worship service itself would take some three or four hours, what with the meal, the Lord's Supper taken in the context of that meal, the discourse of Paulos, the time of witnessing, the singing, the prayers, and the prophesying and speaking in tongues. Camilla reckoned that the guests would not be leaving until late into the evening, and she worried it might be all too much for Erastos, for he was still weak and had lost a good deal of weight over the week. Suddenly Camilla heard her name being called.

"Camilla, I have remembered something," said Erastos, as he walked slowly into the tablinum where she was standing. No one had pressed Erastos on what exactly had happened to him. Camilla figured it would come back to Erastos gradually, over time.

"What is it, dearest?" Camilla wrapped her arms around her husband.

"I certainly did not fall, Camilla. I was hit over the head with a blunt object, some kind of club, and as I was falling to the ground, before I blacked out, I saw a face, a face I had seen several times before."

Camilla sucked in some air and asked, "Who was it?"

"My memory is quite clear. I can still see him in my mind's eye. It was that big ugly hit man, Mercury, who works for Aemilianus."

"You need to be certain about this. As you know, it has legal implications. And this sort of knowledge is dangerous. Obviously someone wanted to have you hit hard—hard enough to put you out of commission for a long time, if not permanently!"

"I know, but my memory is not fuzzy at all on this point. What they were not counting on is a miracle through the hands of our friend Paulos."

"I have a suggestion. Sit on it. Use it as a trump card if you need to later. But I do think you should tell Nicanor."

"Why? What is it to him? He can't have anything to do with this."

"You know how slaves talk, especially when they meet other slaves in the agora. The word on the street is that Nicanor has been made an enormous offer by Aemilianus to do something. I think we must do what we can to retain his services and loyalty. This information will be vital to Nicanor if he is in a quandary about what to do with his life. I wouldn't be surprised, knowing what a nasty piece of work Aemilianus is, that he may have tried to bribe Nicanor into helping him win the election. Maybe by pointing out some weakness we have."

"What weakness might that be?" asked an incredulous Erastos.

"Husband, you really must dust out the cobwebs. What meeting is happening in this house tonight? Is it a meeting of a legal or licit religion, acknowledged by Roma as such?"

These rhetorical questions produced stunned silence on the part of Erastos, as if he had been struck by lightning, or better said, as if suddenly the light had dawned on him. Then he said quietly, "Oh Camilla, you are wise beyond your years. And you are right, especially now that I am running for the office of aedile. I must not only watch my back, I must draw my friends close, and know whom I can trust. I will speak to Nicanor this evening. Last night, as he was leaving, he said he would know more of this Paulos person. I think my healing shook him up pretty badly."

At that very moment Nicanor and his new lodger, Krackus, were on the little balcony that overlooked the street and odeon, enjoying a breakfast of Egyptian fruit and fresh bread. Nicanor

♦ A CLOSER LOOK ♦

Slavery and the Household Codes

The slaves referred to in Paul's household codes in Colossians 3–4, Ephesians 5–6 and Philemon, as well as in 1 Corinthians 7, are domestic servants and agricultural slaves. They are not equivalent to those slaves sent to the mines by the Roman Empire. In general, household slaves tended to be treated much better than those who were not, but as both 1 Corinthians 7:21-22 and Philemon make clear, Paul is all for manumission if possible. Indeed, in Philemon he not only asks for Onesimus's manumission but intimates that if someone is a brother in Christ, he should no longer be a slave. Then too, he is opposed to any Christian selling himself into slavery. And this happened with considerable regularity because most slaves were at least guaranteed food, shelter and clothing, whereas a poor free person had no such security blanket.

This is why Paul in 1 Corinthians 7 says that if someone is not a slave, they should not seek to become one, but rather should "stay as you are." The following picture shows the slave façade found in Corinth, and it reminds us that slaves tended to have identifiable hair styles and dress so they could be recognized in public and distinguished from citizens. The irony is that Roman law, particularly in a Roman colony city, was such that when a slave attained freedom, they also could obtain citizenship and go from a dishonorable status to an honorable one, almost overnight. Such was the case with Nicanor.

If we were to examine Paul's household codes closely, we would discover that his strategy in dealing with slavery is to put the leaven of the gospel into the structure of the Christian household and house-church meetings, and let it work its way. What we see is Paul insisting that Christians who are masters act like Christians first, and this meant all sorts of restrictions on how they treated their slaves. Indeed they are to be treated as persons, and when appropriate, as fellow Christians. By the same token, Paul wants slaves to relate to their masters in a Christian manner. If the master worked out the logical implications of Paul's teaching, he would have to conclude that ultimately manumission was the right Christian way to treat slaves in the long run.

Figure 13.1. Depiction of a household slave serving his master (Istanbul Archaeology Museum)

had been shaken by what he had seen at the house of Erastos the previous evening. And now, in the fresh daylight of this morning, he was asking himself, *Did that really happen?* But his reflective mood was broken by a messenger at the door. It was Nicanor's friend Tyche.

Descending the stairway to the door, Nicanor wondered, *What could this be about?* He had told the family he would come to dinner that evening.

"Master Nicanor, Master Erastos requests urgent counsel with you. Something you need to know has come up." Nicanor nodded and said, "I'll be on my way shortly." Walking back into his house,

Nicanor hollered up the stairwell to Krackus, "Relax for a while. I'll be back soon, and we can attend to some things when I return. I'd like to take you down to the taberna and show you that part of my business." Krackus's voice boomed back in reply, "Right. More of this breakfast for me!" Nicanor smiled. Krackus had the potential to eat him out of house and home.

Nicanor hurried down the street, taking a left on Lechaion Road. In the distance he could hear the voices of the auctioneers in the slave market already at their work, selling off one slave after another, dividing families, breaking hearts, making money. There were loud shouts now and again of, "But that is my child," or "Please do not separate me from my wife, she's pregnant." It reminded Nicanor of his previous life, and it made him wonder again if he shouldn't just *carpe diem* and take the offer of Aemilianus. Today was the day of decision, and he was still uncertain about the matter. The world could be a dark and ugly place, and slavery was one of its more ugly aspects. Should he simply forget he had once been bought by Erastos and separated from his own father? These thoughts were uppermost in his mind as he rushed over to Erastos's villa to hear the latest revelation.

It was Erastos himself who came to the door on this crisp sunny morning. And Nicanor had to admit, here was the visible proof that a miracle did happen last night. Instead of ushering him into the house, Erastos came toward Nicanor and said, "Let's go for a walk in my back garden, as I want you to hear this privately, and without the walls listening."

As they began to walk, Erastos took on a serious tone. "Nicanor, you have been a friend, indeed a member of this household, for a very long time. I am now confiding in you some dangerous information." Nicanor looked at Erastos with surprise. "I now remember clearly what happened to me up near the aqueduct, and it was no accident. I was hit over the head with a blunt object. And I saw as I fell the person who did this to me. You remember that big, ugly guy, a former wrestler, who works for Aemilianus?"

"Mercury?" asked Nicanor.

"Yes, Mercury. It was him, with a club, and I swear this as my God is my witness and on my honor."

What Nicanor had feared to be the case had, in fact, proved to be true. Aemilianus was up to the dirtiest of dirty tricks, and if it had not been for a miracle of healing, he probably would have gotten away with it.

"I must ask you a question, Nicanor. Your life is your own, of course, but my slaves have told me that Aemilianus has made you some sort of enormous offer. Is this true?"

Nicanor hung his head, and then nodded. "Yes, it is true. He even offered to adopt me as his son so I could inherit his estate. I think he is pretty desperate to find an heir. He's almost fifty years old now. And I must give him an answer today."

"And what do you intend to tell him?"

There was a pause as Nicanor looked at the ground. Then he said, "The only honorable thing to do, in light of this most recent revelation, is to tell the man no, but I am under no illusions about what will happen then. Aemilianus will be very angry, and his effort to retaliate will kick into motion. That is why I just hired some muscle—the former gladiator Krackus."

"Smart move. But I have a suggestion for when you go to see Aemilianus later." Then Erastos whispered something in Nicanor's ear that made him smile. With this Nicanor turned to go, but Erastos added, "I didn't want to tell you this before we had talked, but it is my intent, with Camilla's encouragement, to write you into my will. Of course, I will take care of my wife and children, but there is plenty enough to go around and secure everyone's future. I want us to be friends, real friends, not patron and client, from now on. In fact, it is my prayer you may become my brother in Christ, but that is a conversation for another day."

Nicanor did not know how to respond to this, and inside he was berating himself for thinking ill of Erastos, and for even entertaining the idea of getting enmeshed in Aemilianus's web. So he simply said, "Thank you. From the bottom of my heart. I look forward to what is next in our relationship. I must run now."

As Erastos watched him round the side of the villa and hasten down the path, he said to himself, *There goes a man of good character. Julia and Camilla are right about him.*

14

THE AFTERNOON OF
THE DAY OF THE SUN

♦ ♦ ♦

Nicanor had made up his mind to wait until later in the afternoon to go to Aemilianus's villa. For one thing, it was not far from Erastos's place, so he could beat a fast retreat up the hill if he needed to. And for another, he didn't want to make Gordianus and Krackus follow him around all day. He had now dubbed them "the bruise brothers," though truth be told, Gordianus wouldn't harm anyone. Krackus was another story. You couldn't judge a person by his outward appearance.

Having swung by his apartment to pick up Krackus, Nicanor and his friend went by the shop to get Gordianus. The three of them were now headed toward Isthmia and Nicanor's taberna. It was almost comical to see these three traveling down the road together. Nicanor, dwarfed between his two companions, looked for all the world like the little child guarded by his two big brothers.

Along the road they passed many travelers streaming into Corinth from the port. Halfway along their walk they came across a party traveling in a carriage, with one wheel stuck deep in a rut caused by the recent rains. Seeing it, Krackus said, "Let's give them a hand, Gordianus." Nicanor, for his part, was left with the role of assisting the young lady in the carriage as she descended its step. With a deep crimson cloak pulled over her head, her features were well hidden. But when she looked up and saw Nicanor, she gave him a smile that took his breath away. "Thank you so much," she said in a soft voice. "My slaves had not been able to pull me out of the ditch. My name is Alexia. And yours?"

"I am Nicanor. May I ask where you are going?"

"Certainly. We are on our way to Corinth to see my sister and her husband. Perhaps you know them—Camilla and Erastos."

"Know them," exclaimed Nicanor, almost shouting. "I used to be Erastos's slave, and now we are friends who share business interests. I have just returned from Roma to buy some marble for his leitourgia, as he is running for aedile. In fact, I will be going to their house tonight for their dinner, and . . . um . . . 'meeting.'"

"Excellent. So we can make better acquaintance there." By this time, the "bruise brothers" had extricated the back right wheel from the muddy ditch using some leverage and brute force. To finish the job Krackus had single-handedly picked up the rear of the carriage and set it back on the road, with Gordianus admiring his strength. Turning to Nicanor he said, "It's going to be hard to keep that man fed."

For the rest of the journey to the taberna, Nicanor could think of little else than the lovely face and voice of Alexia. Some twenty minutes later the three companions arrived at the Cock Crow, and Nicanor finally snapped back into the present.

"Krackus, here is my modest establishment. It does have one room upstairs that you could use on nights when you have to stay late here. My vision of this, should everything work out and you decide to stick with it, is that you will be my junior partner and perhaps eventually co-owner. We can draw up the paperwork later. I don't want you to simply be the enforcer of civility here, I would like for you to use your contacts at the school and elsewhere to increase the business. We do serve decent food here, and though the wine is not the very best, it is not the dregs either. What we do not want here is prostitutes and prostitution, but otherwise most anyone is welcome. I hear from your fellow pugilists at the school that you have a good head for figures, and so I would expect you to order things and know how far in advance to do so, and how much to order. Of course, the port is just over the hill, so you can make our deals with the ship owners there. And indeed, we need to put up a sign at the port, directing people this way. We have a built-in, though transient clientele, if we just advertise a little bit."

Krackus was beaming by the end of this little speech, and Nicanor knew what must be going through the mind of Gordianus, who had already worked for him for years. Turning to him he said, "And if you are wondering, Gordianus, I would like to make you the same offer of eventual full partnership in our shop in town, and put it in writing. You already have many skills and good ideas about how to increase our business, and with Corinth growing, the need for stone for building will only increase. Thus, I am authorizing you to go down to Lechaeum, where there is an old quarry, and see what is there. Find out who still owns it, as it looks abandoned, and if there is still plenty of stone there, let's make the owner an offer."

Gordianus and Krackus could see that though he had not mentioned any of this before, clearly Nicanor had been thinking about this for some time, thinking ahead, and wisely too. "I cannot speak for Krackus, but I gladly accept this offer," Gordianus said. And Krackus added, "Me too."

Nicanor looked at both goliaths and replied, "Well, I suggest we go inside and see if there is not at least one amphora of the very best wine, and drink to this plan. I love it when a plan comes together." For the next hour the three men drank and talked about the future. By three in the afternoon, however, the sun had begun to slip down the sky. It was now time to make the visit Nicanor had been delaying and dreading, and would rather have avoided altogether. "Time to go, boys," said Nicanor. "We must face Aemilianus. I can't tell you how much I am grateful that you two are going with me. I doubt they will try anything on the spot. But we will have to be vigilant and watch out going forward."

The journey back into Corinth and then heading west toward the home of Marcus Aurelius Aemilianus was a slow one, for the road was clogged with people, carriages, horses and carts. Some thirty minutes into the journey Krackus asked, "Will Aemilianus be expecting you?"

"Oh yes, but he will not be expecting either of you, and all the better for that. The element of surprise will help, I hope."

Aemilianus had spent most of the day with his scribe, catching up on correspondence and business records. With a man as rich as he was, there was much to do, and it was hard to keep up with all his investments. He was fortunate that his scribe was also an excellent accountant as well. But in the back of his mind he wondered why Nicanor had not come sooner on this day, especially if he was eager to consummate the deal. Finally the knock came on the door, and Publius, the body servant, went and opened the door. Publius was in fact a small man and when the door opened a crack, Krackus pushed it wide open and walked in, in front of Nicanor, with Gordianus trailing behind. This caught Aemilianus completely off guard. As was his custom, he allowed his slaves to have some time off toward the end of the day of the sun, and at this point almost no one was home except Publius, Gratia, his wife, and Aemilianus.

"Why all this entourage, Nicanor? Are we not friends?" Aemilianus asked, rising with his hand extended toward Nicanor. But Nicanor did not take his hand. Instead he said, "I have decided not to accept your offer, though it is a very generous one, and I am sure that it will cost me not to do so."

With this, Aemilianus turned scarlet. "You are quite right about that. Nobody turns down an offer from me without great cost."

"Yet, I think, this time, Aemilianus, you will need to reconsider that implied threat," said Nicanor coolly. "For I am here to tell you some other news as well. Erastos is alive and well!" At this Nicanor saw a look of surprise pass over Aemilianus's face.

Pressing on he added, "More to the point, he knows it was your Mercury who tried to bash his head in. It was you who ordered that foul play, you who tried to destroy a good man whom you saw as a rival. It was you who were scheming to have a clear path to the office of aedile, and I am here to tell you that unless you cease and desist from all such hostile behavior toward both Erastos and myself, Erastos is prepared to go to Gallio and report you. Already, he has spoken with his lawyer, and he has drawn up the papers accusing you of assault. He will turn them over to Gallio if you even so much as give a dirty look in his direction or mine. Am I clear?" Nicanor's voice had gotten louder and louder as this speech went on. Emboldened by his companions and the wine, he had said all he wanted to say. And more.

"Yes, you are clear," said a subdued Aemilianus. He knew that even with his pedigree, a public shaming like losing a lawsuit would be bad for his business and would besmirch his family's honor. And he noticed that Nicanor had not said that anyone would be trying to bar him from running for aedile. In his devious mind he was thinking, *There is still time to beat Erastos with a few well-placed bribes of the aedile council.* What he did not know was that Erastos had already thought of this, and had warned his best friend on the council, Octavian, to watch out for it. Forewarned was forearmed.

"May the *better* man win the office of aedile," said Aemilianus.

"To that I can only say, I quite agree." With this, Nicanor turned around and followed Gordianus out the door, with Krackus striding behind.

"Gentlemen, that man is capable of anything. So I must urge both of you to also be vigilant and look out for yourselves in the coming days. I want my new business partners to live long and prosper."

"And you as well," said Gordianus. "Master Nicanor, would it not be wise for one of us to come with you to Erastos's place this evening, and then walk you home? You are, after all, slight of stature."

"Yes, you are right about that," said Nicanor. "Gordianus, you should go home and be with your family. Krackus, if you don't mind, I will ask you to stay. It will take some time, but I am sure

Camilla will gladly welcome you to the meal and the festivities tonight. And if the religious meeting is not to your liking, you can simply wait in the garden or the front of the house for me, and we will go home together. Does that sound like a plan?" And with Gordianus turning around and heading home, Nicanor and Krackus found themselves heading toward the villa of Erastos, both of them realizing they were very hungry.

15

The End of the Day

♦ ♦ ♦

The first thing Nicanor noticed when he arrived at Erastos's house was that it had been decorated with garlands, as if for a special feast or wedding day. Camilla was in the mood to celebrate her husband's recovery, and she had decided to go all out. Already some thirty people were in the house, milling around the impluvium, the atrium and the courtyard in the center of the villa complex. Torches had been rigged on poles in the courtyard, and people were enjoying all sorts of rich appetizers, including imported Lucrene oysters and the best Falernian wine. Krackus remarked, "Your friends really know how to throw a party."

At about the twelfth hour, all the guests had finally arrived, sixty-five of them, including Camilla's sister, Alexia. She looked truly stunning in her long, flowing, deep blue gown, with the torch flames flickering across her face.

Once all had gathered, Erastos, dressed in his finest toga, trimmed with a slight royal purple border, asked Paulos if he would step into the atrium and offer a prayer of blessing on the evening. The air was crisp and cool, and when Nicanor looked up into the sky he saw an infinity of stars and a huge orange moon rising. Tomorrow, the day of the moon, would in fact be the day when the moon would be full.

Paulos was dressed in his rough woolen cloak, the signature winter garb of this wiry man who had grown up in the warmer clime of Judea. He stood up, and in a strong voice, with a slight accent, said in Greek, "Most high God, Lord Jesus Christ, Holy Spirit, we invoke your presence in this place, and ask that you would fill all here with your presence. As we come to worship you this evening, through word and breaking bread and sharing in the Lord's table and singing and celebration, we are especially glad for the recovery of this good man Erastos, who has opened his home for our meeting. Bless this food to our good, and us to your service, in your Son's name." After which many there present added the Jewish word meaning "so be it," *amen.*

Coming over to Nicanor, and bringing her sister with her, Camilla gave Nicanor the kiss of greeting and said, "My sister has been telling me that you have rescued her today."

"Well, actually it was more like Krackus, who is sitting over there on the impluvium, slurping down oysters, and another of my employees, Gordianus, who did that."

"Nevertheless, I do not believe in chance, Nicanor, or mere luck. I believe the one God works all things together for good for those who love him. Do you know why Alexia has come to town?"

"I presume to visit you, of course."

Taking Nicanor aside into the small sitting room off the impluvium, she added in a quiet voice, "Yes, that is true, but with the death of my father some months ago, Alexia has nowhere left to stay in Roma. Our brothers have inherited the estate, and so she has come here, in hopes of making a life in Corinth. I have

Figure 15.1. A view inside the front doorway of a villa with the impluvium (rain-catching pool) in the foreground and peristyle (courtyard) in the distance

tasked Erastos with the job of finding her a husband—finally! The problem has been our family did not have enough money for a good dowry for both her and myself, and since I was the older, I got married first. Then our family fell on hard times when Claudius became Emperor, and the taxes skyrocketed. In any case, Erastos will be looking for a proper match for Alexia, and if you know anyone who might be suitable, please let him know."

With this she winked at Nicanor, and his face went bright red. She added, "We need another enterprising good man in the family, preferably one who knows the Lord Jesus."

Nicanor somewhat awkwardly told these ladies what an honor it was to be with them both, and then said, "I have promised little Julia I would tell her a bedtime story, so if you will excuse me, I must do that now and then return for the next course of the dinner."

Beating a fast retreat, Nicanor walked swiftly down the main corridor of the house to Julia's room, and found that her nurse, Ariadne, was there with her, keeping watch, lest she burst out of the room and run into the dinner. She had already had her dinner and was in her nighttime apparel, for she normally went to bed before the third hour of the night. The first words out of her mouth when she saw Nicanor was, "Did you meet my aunt Alexia? She is beautiful."

Nicanor coughed, and said, "Yes, she is, but I promised I would come and tell you a bedtime story, and so I shall. Ariadne, you are welcome to stay, or stand just out in the hall, as this will only take a little time."

"Ah, I was hoping for a long story," said Julia with a pout.

"Not tonight, as I am supposed to go have dinner shortly. Perhaps another night. Tonight we will hear the story of Persephone. Do you remember this story?"

"Only a little. Please use all those different voices you use to tell the story. I like that." Julia smiled as she snuggled in close to Nicanor.

"First, you need to know that Persephone is only this beautiful maiden's Greek name. Her Roman name may be more familiar to you, Proserpine."

"Ah yes, was she not queen of the underworld?"

"Yes, little one, but you are jumping ahead of the story, and some of versions of this story say it is not safe to pronounce her name, lest something deadly befall you. But that is just a myth, I'm sure. In any case, Persephone was the daughter of Zeus and Demeter, but there came a day when she was stolen as a little girl from her mother's side by Hades, the god of the underworld, who longed to have her for a wife. She was innocently picking flowers one day, when Hades snuck up and abducted her."

"Bad Hades," said Julia. "He tried to snatch my pater as well, but Paulos saved him."

"Yes, you are right," said Nicanor. "Now Demeter was the goddess of the earth, and all fertility, the ruler of all growing things, and in her grief for her daughter she ceased allowing things to grow on the earth, and the earth became very barren.

"Finally Zeus got tired of hearing the cries of the humans who had nothing to eat and the weeping of Demeter, and decided to do something about it. Zeus forced Hades to return Persephone. But the Fates had decreed that whoever had something to eat or drink in the underworld had to stay there forever. Hermes was sent to retrieve Persephone, but before she was released, Hades fooled her into eating some pomegranate seeds. And so each year Persephone had to return to spend the winter in the underworld. That's why nothing grows in the wintertime while Persephone lives below. But come the Ides of March, she returns, and so does life to the earth, through the joy and celebration of Demeter, who has gotten her daughter back once again."

"So this story explains the origin of winter?"

"That's right. You are such a smart girl."

"Mater says it is a nice story, but only a myth, and that we need a religion based on what is real, not in myths. What do you think?"

"I think your mother is a wise woman, and now I must leave and go eat. Sleep well, little Julia, and I will see you again soon." He kissed her good night on the forehead, pulled her blanket up to her chin and quietly slipped out the door.

The meal, in fact, had moved on to the third course, and people were eating everywhere, standing, sitting, in the courtyard, in the tablinum. Everywhere. Krackus had seated himself at Erastos's desk in the tablinum and was devouring chicken wings, one after another. "This food is excellent," said Krackus. "We must come here more often."

"Nicanor!" called Camilla. "We have reserved a place of honor for you on the couch next to Erastos and Paulos. You must come into the triclinium."

Pulling up his toga so he could sit and then recline on the couch, Nicanor found himself sitting directly opposite Camilla and Alexia, who were on the same couch. In front of him was a table filled with food. Grabbing a plate, he took some fruit, chicken, leeks and another goblet of the delicious wine.

"You have really gone all out tonight, Camilla," he said, raising his goblet to her.

"And with every reason. My husband is well, my sister is here. The prospects look good that Erastos may get elected aedile, and winter will soon be over." The meal went through several more courses, but toward the end of it, Paulos sat up on his couch and said, "Everyone, it is time as we draw the meal to a close, to share together in the Lord's Supper with this last cup of wine, and with this special unleavened woven bread that Camilla has baked for the occasion. It is time for us to turn our attention to our Lord."

Raising the bread first, and then the cup, Paulos said, "For I received from the Lord what I also passed on to you: the Lord Jesus, on the night he was betrayed, took bread, and when he had given thanks, he broke it and said, 'This is my body, which is for you; do this in remembrance of me.'

"In the same way, after supper he took the cup, saying, 'This cup is the new covenant in my blood; do this, whenever you drink it, in remembrance of me.' For whenever you eat this bread and drink this cup, you proclaim the Lord's death until he comes.

"So then, whoever eats the bread or drinks the cup of the Lord in an unworthy manner will be guilty of sinning against the body and blood of the Lord. Everyone ought to examine themselves before they eat of the bread and drink from the cup. For those who eat and drink without discerning the body of Christ eat and drink judgment on themselves. That is why some among you are weak and sick, and a number of you have fallen asleep.

"But if we were more discerning with regard to ourselves, we would not come under such judgment. Nevertheless, when we are judged in this way by the Lord, we are being disciplined so that we will not be finally condemned with the world. So then, my brothers and sisters, when you gather to eat, you should all eat together as we have done on this night, with all waiting for one another to dine together." This last instruction was a reminder that some of the slaves from the other house churches usually came a bit late, after they had finished their work, and Paulos wanted them to be treated as equals at this meal, part of the whole group's sharing of it in common, not those who got the leftovers after the fact.

At this juncture Paulos broke the large woven bread, and told each person to take a piece and hold it until all had their bread. Once this transpired, he then passed around the cup, telling each person to dip their bread in the cup and partake of it together. He then said, holding up his wine-stained morsel, "Because we are all one body, we all partake of one and the same loaf, and drink from one and the same cup." With this, they all consumed their bit of wine-soaked bread, including Nicanor and Krackus. They were not about to break the religious protocols, for one thing they had learned growing up with Greek religion, if the ritual was not observed perfectly by all, it had to be done all over again since a sacrilege had been committed. And indeed, Nicanor had taken Paulos to be warning against such sacrilege. But he really did not understand why the bread and wine were called the body and blood of Jesus. Perhaps that would be explained later.

Just at that juncture, two of the household servants entered with lyres in their hands, and began to play. Paulos told the group, "We will now all sing together a hymn to Christ our God." Then, led by the two young slaves with their tenor voices, one and all began to sing.

"Christ who, being in very nature God,
did not consider equality with God something
    to be used to his own advantage;
rather, he made himself nothing
by taking the very nature of a servant,
being made in human likeness.
And being found in appearance as a human being,
he humbled himself
by becoming obedient to death—
even death on a cross!

"Therefore God exalted him to the highest place
and gave him the name that is above every name,
that at the name of Jesus every knee should bow,
in heaven and on earth and under the earth,

and every tongue acknowledge that Jesus Christ is Lord,
to the glory of God the Father."

Nicanor had not known what to expect, he was just along for
the ride. Or so he thought. But listening to the singing of songs,
with various melodies and even some harmonies, was wonderful,
as the voices rose into the night air. This was not like the keening
and moaning and intoning and chanting he had heard in temples,
but rather the singing of songs with intelligible lyrics, though
often he did not understand what they were talking about, especially the stuff about Jesus rising from the dead. Music had
seldom moved him so much. And the last song, which was especially winsome, found him wiping his eyes with his sleeve.

Of course he knew the tales of gods coming to earth dis-
guised as humans, like the stories about Zeus and Hermes visiting Lystra, but would a god not only take on the form of a
servant, but submit to a rebellious slave's death on a cross? This
sounded like foolishness to Nicanor. And what was that second
verse about? Would the most high God really exalt and praise
this person Christ for dying on a cross? It was one thing to
make a hero like Herakles a demi-god. But a Jew like this Jesus?
This totally inverted the normal notions of honor and shame,
and of what the gods thought was praiseworthy behavior.

Nicanor was going to have to ask some questions about these
things, but now his curiosity was piqued. The one question that
presented itself immediately was, "How could such loving and
honest and kind people, who otherwise seemed in their right
minds and not prone to religious mania, believe such a tale?
Unless of course there is some sort of compelling evidence that
it is true." Nicanor had seen a miracle, but he was not sure he

was prepared to believe in a literal resurrection of a crucified and dead Jew, much less his apotheosis and exaltation to the right hand of the most high God. That seemed to stretch credulity beyond the breaking point.

At this juncture, Camilla announced, "What we will do now is adjourn to the courtyard, where we have not only torches but braisers to keep us warm. There Paulos will address us and we will worship some more, in spirit and in truth. And we will await the Spirit to prompt the prophets and prophetesses to speak."

Paulos stood in the middle of the courtyard with all those present circled around him, some holding torches. It was, of course, customary after a meal to have wine, and to have an after-dinner speaker. And some of those present had refilled and brought their goblets with them into the courtyard, prepared to listen. Even Krackus did so, and he was expecting an entertaining speech, perhaps in the form of epideictic rhetoric. Nicanor really wasn't sure what to expect.

Holding out his hand in the gesture of an orator, Paulos began:

"On this night of celebration and joy over the recovery of Erastos, it is only appropriate that we praise God by speaking of one of his chief attributes, his main virtues that he also instills in all those who believe in him. I am referring of course to *agape*, unconditional, free and gracious love, loving with no implied requirement of return. It is a sort of love many of us here have experienced in our relationship with the risen Lord Jesus, and would long for all to experience, for it is the one quality of life and relationships that is most enduring and endearing, and can most mold us into the image of Christ himself. I myself have found this to be true, even in the midst of great personal loss and

♦ A CLOSER LOOK ♦

Rhetoric—The Ancient Art
of Persuasion

Public speaking was a refined art by the time of the Empire, and indeed Greek rhetoric had been part of basic and upper-level education since the time of Aristotle. Most ancient persons, wherever they lived in the Empire, were either producers or consumers of the ancient art of rhetoric. In these largely oral cultures, the art of oral persuasion was far more important and pervasively influential than inscriptions or decrees or letters. Indeed, letters in the Greco-Roman world largely conformed to the conventions of rhetoric, and it was only in Paul's day that letters had begun to take on certain set conventions of form. Rhetoric, on the other hand, had enjoyed established orders and forms for centuries.

There were three major types of ancient rhetoric. (1) There was the rhetoric of attack and defense, which focused on the past. This was forensic rhetoric, the rhetoric of lawyers and law courts. (2) There was the rhetoric of advice and consent, which focused on the future, deliberative rhetoric, the rhetoric of the ancient Greek *ekklesia*, or democratic assembly. It is likely no accident that Paul called his house churches *ekklesiai*, since they were places where deliberative persuasion and advice would be given. (3) Finally, there was epideictic rhetoric, the rhetoric of praising or blaming someone or something in the present. This was a frequent and popular form of rhetoric, which was heard in the agora or after dinner at a banquet and as an encomium at a funeral. On nights like this night of celebration and praising God for Erastos's recovery, epideictic rhetoric was in order.

suffering. Indeed, this sort of love, even above brotherly or sisterly love, must be seen as the greatest quality and expression any life can exhibit. So I ask you to bear with me friends for a while, as I extol this sort of love." With this *exordium*, Paulos began to speak in a more lyrical and poetic manner.

"If I speak in human or angelic tongues, but do not have love, I am only a resounding gong or a clanging cymbal (like those made at the bronze works here in Corinth). If I have the gift of prophecy and can fathom all mysteries and all knowledge, and if I have a faith that can move mountains, but do not have love, I am nothing. If I give all I possess to the poor and give over my body to hardship that I may boast, but do not have love, I gain nothing.

"Love is patient, love is kind. It does not envy, it does not boast, it is not proud. It does not dishonor others, it is not self-seeking, it is not easily angered, it keeps no record of wrongs. Love does not delight in evil but rejoices with the truth. It always protects, always trusts, always hopes, always perseveres.

"Love never fails. But where there are prophecies, they will cease; where there are tongues, they will be stilled; where there is knowledge, it will pass away. For we know in part and we prophesy in part, but when completeness comes, what is in part disappears.

"When I was a child, I talked like a child, I thought like a child, I reasoned like a child. When I became a man, I put the ways of childhood behind me. For now we see only a reflection as in a mirror; then we shall see face to face. Now I know in part; then I shall know fully, even as I am fully known. And now these three remain: faith, hope and love. But the greatest of these is love.

"Look around you now, friends, have you not seen and felt this love in this very household and from this very family? Have you not experienced it in good times and in bad, when someone was well or ill? When you have experienced such love as Christ pours into your life and into your very hearts, you know it and cannot deny it. It is so true, so real, so pure, and it transforms those loving as well as those being loved profoundly. The love of human beings is fickle, uncertain, intermittent. Not so the love of God which he longs to share with us all. While we were yet sinners, Christ died for us, so that we might live in such love, live in newness of life. It is what God created all humans for—to be loved, and to love.

"And so on this night of nights, I appeal to your hearts—let love in, let Christ in if you have not already done so. It is not merely the key to a joyful and genuine life, a life full of purpose and meaning. It is the key to eternity, to everlasting life. Amen."

And many in the assembly replied with hearty "amens" as well.

Nicanor found himself moved beyond words by this oration, and he could see many in the circle that surrounded Paulos wiping their eyes. Paulos might look like a crooked-backed old shopkeeper, but he had words that moved even the skeptical and hardhearted. Nicanor deeply and desperately wanted such love in his life, but this whole evening had raised many more questions than it had answered, and just when he thought everything was about to draw to a close, something else happened.

Both men and women started speaking in a language he had never heard before, and rather quickly Paulos interrupted and asked, "Is there anyone here tonight with the gift of interpreting these tongues? If not, we must move on to the prophesying, which all can understand, so all may worship with both their spirit and their mind."

Figure 15.2. The temple of the oracle at Delphi, where the Greek practice of prophecy became famous

What surprised Nicanor most about what happened next was that prophecies were directed to very specific situations and persons. For example, there was a prophecy spoken about Erastos, which said, "You have been spared for a specific reason: to serve the Lord faithfully in the world, while not being of the world. Always remember your healing and remain faithful."

This, thought Nicanor, was apt. But at this point he felt more like an outside observer of someone else's religion. That is, until Camilla herself came up to Nicanor and led him to the middle of the gathered meeting. And then it was that something both frightening and exhilarating—and confusing—happened.

Camilla closed her eyes, opened her mouth and began speaking in a voice that seemed deeper and more authoritative than her own. "Nicanor, thus says the Lord Jesus to you: 'It is time, time indeed for you to repent of your skepticism, for you

♦ A CLOSER LOOK ♦

Prophecy in First-Century Corinth

One of the problems with interpreting a passage like 1 Corinthians 14 is that while we can get directly at some of the things Paul thought about prophecy, we need also to understand how the Corinthians were viewing it. For example, how did they view the relationship of ecstasy and prophecy? How much did the previous experience of Gentile Christians with prophecy at Delphi or the temple of Apollo affect the way they viewed or practiced prophecy in the Christian worship service?

The most important thing to say and to know about Greek prophecy at Delphi and elsewhere is that it was consultative prophecy. In other words, it was given in response to questions and requests of various sorts. This is likely why some women in the Corinthian church had been asking questions of the prophets and prophetesses and also why Paul asked them to be silent and ask questions at home. Christian worship was not intended to degenerate into a question-and-answer session. Rather prophecy in the biblical tradition was a top-down matter—God had something to say to his people, rather than his people having something to ask their deity.

Paul, for his part, believed that the prophecies of Christians should be weighed and sifted, because they could be 80 percent inspiration and 20 percent perspiration. This is why he warned in Romans 12 that each prophet should only prophesy according to the measure of his or her faith, and not beyond that. But doubtless in the euphoria of the moment, prophets did at times get carried away, just as preachers do today. More importantly, it is clear from the end of 1 Corinthians 14 that Paul saw his own speech as prophetic, with the same authority as a command of the Lord.

What we learn from a closer examination of 1 Corinthians 11–14, includes the following: (1) Prophecy is not preaching since it is not an exposition of a preexisting sacred text but rather a late word from God. It is an intelligible phenomenon that does not require the sort of interpretation tongues does. (2) The function of prophecy is edification, exhortation and consolation (1 Cor 14:3). (3) First Corinthians 14:25 suggests that prophecy could also involve insight into a present problem or even the present condition of someone's heart. (4) Prophecy is a gift all Christians could and should seek from God, though the Spirit determines who gets which gift (14:1). (5) While Paul distinguishes prophecy from praying or teaching (see 1 Cor 11 and 12:29), nonetheless prophecy does have a didactic function (14:19). (6) Perhaps most importantly, the authority lay in the word and in the Spirit inspiring the word, not in the vessel or instrument speaking that word. If something human was added to an inspired word, that had to be discerned and sifted out during the weighing of the prophecies, and not attributed to the divine source. (7) Prophecy was a gift that both men and women exercised in early Christianity, and there is no reason to think Paul expected that gift to be confined to the apostolic age. Indeed, 1 Corinthians 13 suggests it will continue until faith becomes sight when the Lord returns. It seems then that the new prophecies in the New Testament era mainly served the purposes of exhorting or exegeting particular persons and situations and churches, and thus much of it was not preserved for all eternity, nor did it become a part of the canon. It offered a timely truth rather than a timeless one.

have seen my works of healing in the life of Erastos, and you have known my mercy as I watched over you as you travelled from Roma, and you have begun to prosper in life, but alas, your heart longs for love, and your house has no wife or children to welcome you home, today, tomorrow or ever. You have a noble and honest character, but still there is an absence or void in your soul that only I, Jesus, the risen one, can fill. It is time for your life to be ruled by a sound faith rather than by your fears and desires and your human wisdom. Even little Julia knows me, and yet you with all your wisdom do not.'"

Trembling, and weeping, and with his stomach all in knots, Nicanor sensed he was in the presence of something holy and he broke down. He could not silence the questions in his mind, but his heart longed to respond in some way to the prophecy. Just then Nicanor felt a hand on his head, and then another, and another, and then one on his right shoulder and one on his left shoulder, and all around him there was powerful praying going on. Suddenly there was a tiny hand that slipped into his, the hand of a child. She whispered to Nicanor, "We all love you here." And she gave him her biggest hug. Quite unexpectedly Nicanor felt warmth coursing through his body, and he ceased shaking, ceased weeping. It was love. Turning to Camilla and Erastos, he smiled and hugged them as well, and said "I would learn more of this god Jesus. I have many, many questions. But if Jesus is anything like your loving family, it will be worth all the time in the world to learn of him."

Post Scriptum

♦ ♦ ♦

There are two famous inscriptions from Roman Corinth that mention Erastos. Both are in Latin. One, which probably comes from the late Claudian or early Nero period, reads: "Erastus for the office of aedile laid this pavement at his own expense." It is found in front of the large theater at Corinth, still in situ where it was discovered. The second inscription reads "The Vitelli, Frontius, and Erastus, dedicate this . . ."[1]

Figure P.1. Erastus inscription at Corinth

---

[1]On all this see my *Conflict and Community in Corinth*, pp. 32-34.

Here we likely have one of those rare synchronisms between artifacts and inscriptions on the one hand, and the New Testament on the other. In my judgment, it is hardly likely that there were two Erasti who were aediles in the 50s in Corinth when Paul was there and just afterward. No, the two inscriptions refer to one and the same Erastos. And in Romans 16:23, writing from Corinth, Paul sends the greetings of Erastos, the *oikonomos tēs poleōs*, Greek for "aedile of the city." All of this raises the interesting question of how a high-status Christian like Erastos managed to function, including helping maintain pagan temples, all the while keeping his new faith. In short, the story in this book, while fiction, is based in the historical realities of the Corinthian Christian community that Paul founded.

Image Credits and Permissions

Figure 1.1. Andrei Nacu/Wikimedia Commons

Figures 1.2, 1.3, 1.4, 2.2, 2.3, 2.4, 4.4, 6.1, 6.3, 6.4, 6.5, 9.1, 9.2, 10.1, 11.1, 13.1, 15.1, 15.2, P.1. Used by permission of Mark R. Fairchild, Ph.D.; Huntington University, Huntington, IN.

Figure 2.5. inyucho/Flickr. Used under the Creative Commons License, Attribution 2.0.

Figure 3.1. Used courtesy of Judy Hamblen.

Figure 3.2. This photo was taken May 31, 2011 by David J. Lull, Professor of New Testament, Wartburg Theological Seminary, Dubuque, IA. Used courtesy of the photographer.

Figure 4.1. PureCore/Wikimedia Commons

Figure 4.2. Used courtesy of Classical Numismatic Group, Inc., <www.cngcoins.com>.

Figure 4.3. Used courtesy of Joe Geranio/cngcoins.com.

Figure 6.2. Overbeck/Wikimedia Commons

Figure 8.1. Overbeck/Wikimedia Commons

Figure 8.2. Matthias Kabel/Wikimedia Commons

Figure 9.3. © 2011 by Jinx Mim <http://jinxmim.deviantart.com/art/Curule-Chairs-205091063>.

Figure 9.4. Flanker/Wikimedia Commons